SECOND EDITION

A SHORT GUIDE TO ACTION RESEARCH

ANDREW P. JOHNSON
Minnesota State University, Mankato

PEARSON

Boston ■ New York ■ San Francisco
Mexico City ■ Montreal ■ Toronto ■ London ■ Madrid ■ Munich ■ Paris
Hong Kong ■ Singapore ■ Tokyo ■ Cape Town ■ Sydney

Senior Editor: Arnis E. Burvikovs
Series Editorial Assistant: Megan Smallidge
Marketing Manager: Tara Whorf
Editorial-Production Service: Omegatype Typography, Inc.
Composition Buyer: Linda Cox
Manufacturing Buyer: Andrew Turso
Cover Administrator: Rebecca Krzyzaniak
Electronic Composition: Omegatype Typography, Inc.

For related titles andsupport materials, visit our online catalog at www.ablongman.com.

Between the time Website information is gathered and then published, it is not unusual for some sites to have closed. Also, the transcription of URLs can result in typographical errors. The publisher would appreciate notification where these errors occur so that they may be corrected in subsequent editions.

Library of Congress Cataloging-in-Publication Data

Johnson, Andrew P. (Andrew Paul)
    A short guide to action research / Andrew P. Johnson.
       p.   cm.
    Includes bibliographical references.
    ISBN 0-205-41253-X (alk. paper)
     1. Action research in education.   I. Title.

   LB1028.24.J65   2005
   370'.72—dc22

                                        2004043665

Printed in the United States of America

10 9 8 7 6   09 08 07 06

This book is dedicated to my mother, Berdella Johnson,
who first introduced me to the joy and magic of reading.

CONTENTS

CHAPTER EIGHT

Methods of Collecting Data   61

CHAPTER NINE

Methods of Analyzing Data   81

CHAPTER TEN

Quantitative Design in Action Research   93

CHAPTER ELEVEN

Discussion: Your Plan of Action   103

PREFACE

The most important variable in determining the quality of our children's educational experience is the teacher standing in front of a classroom. As such, it is a wise investment to spend time and resources to help teachers become knowledgeable practitioners and to create the conditions whereby they are able to make informed, research-based decisions. Action research is one of the most practical, effective, and economically efficient methods in this regard. This book takes you through all phases of the action research process. My hope is that it can be used as an agent of change.

Action research is a systematic inquiry into one's own practice. The process can be a very important part of the professional growth and development of both preservice and inservice teachers. This book describes how to conduct and report action research. I have endeavored to write in a style that is concise, informative, reader friendly, and to the point. In so doing, I am modeling the style best used in writing action research reports.

I have included activities at the end of each chapter that are designed to reinforce the concepts described therein. If you are reading this book as part of a class, these activities might be used as weekly assignments. If you are reading this book independently, these activities might serve as a vehicle with which to practice or experiment with different ideas and skills related to action research. Good luck to you.

This is the second edition of this action research book. Like the first edition, I have tried to keep things as short and as simple as possible. Too often in educational practice and scholarly work, we mistake quantity and complexity for rigor and effectiveness. I do not want to make this mistake.

NEW TO THIS EDITION

In this second edition I have made four changes: First, there are new samples included in various parts of this text. Second, information related to writing and reporting action research has been changed to reflect the fifth edition of the APA Style Manual. Third, I have included a new chapter, Chapter 2: Research Paradigms and the Nature of Reality. This chapter takes a philosophical look at our assumptions about the nature of reality and how these affect our perceptions of research and ultimately our educational practices. And finally, I've written a new chapter that describes some simple quantitative methodology and analysis that can be used with action research projects.

ACKNOWLEDGMENTS

I wish to thank editor Arnis Burvikovs for his suggestions and work on this project, as well as the reviewers for this edition: Barbara O'Byrne, Marshall University and Gail M. Slater, New York University and New York City Department of Education. Also, I wish to thank those graduate students and classroom teachers who have embraced the ideas described in this text and put them to practical use. Your dedication to education and your determination to move the field of education forward is truly inspiring.

ABOUT THE AUTHOR

Dr. Andrew Johnson is professor and chair of the Department of Educational Studies: Special Populations at Minnesota State University, Mankato in Mankato, Minnesota. He specializes in holistic education, spiritual intelligence, literary instruction, strategies for the inclusive classroom, and gifted education. He is also Codirector of the Center for Talent Development, where he teaches courses related to gifted education. Before moving into higher education, he worked for 9 years in the public schools as a second grade teacher, wrestling coach, volleyball coach, and as a gifted education coordinator. Currently, his areas of interest include spirituality in education, spiritual intelligence, action research, thinking skills, and academic and creative writing. He can be reached for comment at:

Department of Educaitonal Studies: Special Populations
313 Armstrong Hall
Minnesota State University, Mankato
Mankato, MN 56001
andrew.johnson@mnsu.edu
www.coled.mnsu.edu/departments/specpop/ajohnson.htm

SECTION I

RATIONALE

SCIENCE, RESEARCH, AND TEACHING

This book describes how to conduct action research in an educational setting. This chapter contains a description of the nature of science, research, and teaching, all of which are complementary parts of the same pursuit of truth.

SCIENCE

Ask somebody what he or she associates with science. That person is likely to respond with something like biology, astronomy, physics, or chemistry. However, science is not solely a body of knowledge or a particular content area; rather, it includes the processes used to examine and organize the world around us (Johnson, 2000). To engage in the process of science means to look, to seek to understand or know, to guess and test guesses, to create order from chaos, and to develop concepts. Science is "a way of thinking about and observing the universe that leads to a deep understanding of its workings" (Stanovich, 1992, p. 9).

Scientists are simply those who ask questions and find answers. In fact, we all use science in some way each day. Our questions might be as grand as, How did our universe begin? or as mundane as, Which line at the grocery store checkout is faster? or, I wonder what kind of response my new haircut will generate? Teachers are natural scientists. They engage in a form of science when they ask questions such as, How will this new teaching technique work? How are Sally's reading skills coming along? How can I help Billy learn long division?

Science and Pseudoscience

As consumers of scientific inquiry related to education, we must be aware of the differences between science and pseudoscience. Science uses perceived reality to determine beliefs. That is, data are collected to determine what is believed. Pseudoscience uses beliefs to determine perceived reality. One starts with a strong belief, then looks for data to support that belief (see Figure 1.1). Pseudoscience is often used by companies, groups, or individuals to demonstrate that their product, method, or ideology is the most effective or best. Science provides an honest analysis of the situation and is much preferred to pseudoscience.

Science

perceived reality ⟶ determines ⟶ belief

Pseudoscience

belief ⟶ determines ⟶ perceived reality

FIGURE 1.1   Science and Pseudoscience

An example of pseudoscience is the type of "research" that is included with some of the phonics programs advertised on television, which are guaranteed to improve children's reading scores, usually with some snappy, new method. Before you believe these claims, however, consider this: more than a million teachers in our country and thousands of professors have been looking for effective ways to teach children to read for years. If some secret key or magic method was superior to all others, the mathematical odds alone dictate that one of us would have found it by now and published many books and articles describing it.

An example of real science in education is the information published by the National Assessment of Educational Progress (NAEP), which is a part of the U.S. Department of Education. A representative sample of 30,000 students across the United States are selected at random for study (National Center for Educational Statistics, 1998). The kinds of tests, measures, and interviews given to this group are held constant across time and region. That is, a standardized math test given in 1970 in Georgia is similar in content, form, and length to one given in California in 2000 so that comparisons can be made. Thus, we are able to track the progress of U.S. students with some accuracy over time and place.

It is interesting to note that, although many improvements are still needed for our schools, they are not in the miserable state of decay that some groups claim (McQuillan, 1998). When looking at basic skills, scores have remained constant or even risen slightly over the last 25 years (see Table 1.1). This is rather remarkable when one considers the influx of cultures and the many changes in our society, which have included an increase in drug use and violence. On the whole, U.S.

TABLE 1.1   NAEP Average Scores on Standardized Test (500 points possible)

	SCIENCE		MATH		READING	
	1971	*1999*	*1973*	*1999*	*1970*	*1999*
Age 9	225	229	219	232	208	212
Age 13	255	256	266	276	255	259
Age 17	305	295	304	308	285	288

teachers are doing a very good job. However, NAEP shows that while basic skills have remained constant over the years, scores on tasks calling for higher-level thinking have dropped (Routmann, 1996). This contradicts the call for schools to get back to the basics, to have a standardization of process and product in education, and to engage in more testing. These are the kinds of remedies that are thrust on our children when pseudoscience is used to make important educational decisions.

RESEARCH

Scientific knowledge is a body of knowledge generated by research. Research is a way of seeing, a procedure used to view and re-view the world in order to understand it. Research is the systematic method used to collect data to answer questions. The systematic method used by the researcher is the lens through which the world is viewed. Different research methods or lenses provide different views of reality. A variety of scientific methods are used to study the unknown (Hodson, 1988; Stanovich, 1992); however, these methods tend to be put into two broad categories: quantitative and qualitative. Transcendental methodology, a third type of research method, is mentioned in Chapter 2, but an examination of this is beyond the scope of this current text.

Quantitative Research

In quantitative research, sometimes called experimental research, the researcher takes an active role in setting up an observation or experiment to isolate a variable. A variable is the quality or condition about which the researcher wants to draw conclusions. The goal of experimental research is to figure out what the effect of a particular approach or treatment (variable) might be. In order to make an accurate prediction or to demonstrate a causal relationship, the researcher creates an environment that isolates a particular variable by controlling all the extraneous variables. Some important terms in understanding quantitative research follow:

1. The *independent variable* is the treatment or factor that the researcher manipulates to determine a particular effect. It is what is done or not done to a group of people, animals, plants, or things.
2. The *dependent variable* is the particular result or the effect of the treatment. An easy way to remember the distinction between these two variables is to think of the dependent variable as depending on the treatment or independent variable.
3. The *treatment group* or experimental group is the group of subjects, participants, or objects that are exposed to the particular treatment.
4. The *control group* is a group as similar as possible in all characteristics to the treatment group; however, this group is not exposed to the particular treatment for the purposes of comparison.
5. The *research question* is that for which the researcher seeks to find an answer.

6. The *hypothesis* is a tentative statement that can be supported if the outcome of the experimentation is as expected. If a number of different tests continue to support that hypothesis, it may be elevated to the status of theory.

7. A *theory* is an interrelated set of concepts that is used to explain a body of data (Stanovich, 1992). Most hypotheses never make it to the level of theory because it takes a great deal of evidence to support a hypothesis before it can be viewed as valid.

To better understand this process, I have created a mock experiment. This mock experiment is purposely simplistic and exaggerated to demonstrate clearly the salient aspects of quantitative research.

The Coffee Study.   I wanted to find out whether drinking coffee (independent variable) would lead to higher student test scores on standardized achievement tests (dependent variable). To do this, I set up an experimental world in which two relatively similar groups of people had the same experience except for the independent variable. I randomly selected 200 college students and put them into two groups: Group A was the treatment group; Group B was the control group. Group A students were administered the treatment, which in this case was five cups of coffee each day. Group B students were not given coffee. The research question was, Does coffee improve students' performance on standardized tests? My hypothesis was, Drinking coffee improves students' ability to perform on standardized tests. The goal of this study was to prove or disprove my hypothesis.

A standardized test was given as a pretest measure to both groups to determine whether they were relatively equal at the beginning of the experiment. (If all the smart people happened to end up in the treatment group, this would confound the experiment and lead to a false conclusion.) For this experiment to be valid, I needed a sample size that was large enough to conclude that the results were not due to coincidence. The number depends on the research question, but in education, 30 is often seen as the minimum number of subjects needed in each group for a quantitative research study. Of course more subjects are usually better than fewer subjects.

Next, I created a controlled environment in which everything about the two groups was exactly the same except for the independent variable (coffee). In this way, the independent variable (coffee) could be isolated and I could say for certain that coffee did or did not affect the dependent variable (scores on standardized achievement tests). For this to happen, I put the subjects in a biosphere and gave each group controlled doses of study time, food, sleep, television, social interaction, and emotional stress.

In this exaggerated experiment you can begin to see one of the problems with controlled experimental research dealing with human subjects: Manipulating reality makes it nonreality. By controlling the environment I am creating an unreal world. Data from this unreal world is then used to make conclusions about the real world. This is not to suggest, however, that empirical data from quantitative research studies are not valid, but rather that the research method used should be determined by the research question. In this case, the research method is the best possible one to use in specifically answering my research question. However, if I wanted to understand why, when, or where college students drink coffee, I would need to use qualitative methods (discussed in the next section).

In this make-believe coffee experiment, I kept the two groups in their controlled environments long enough for the treatment effect to show up. In this case, it was 2 months. At the end of the treatment, I tested the two groups. These posttest scores were then compared to see whether one group's average was significantly higher than the other's. I also looked at the difference between pretest and posttest scores to see whether one group's gain score was significantly greater than the other's. Statistical procedures were then used to figure out whether the difference between the two groups was statistically significant. This means that the difference is larger than could reasonably be expected by chance or that it could not have happened by coincidence. Table 1.2 shows the results of this experiment.

The results show that the treatment group outperformed the control group by 17% on posttest measures. We will assume this difference is statistically significant. (I do not want to get into a description of statistical analysis here.) It appears that coffee does have a positive effect in students' ability to perform on standardized achievement tests. These results may transfer into other areas of academic performance. However, even in experimental research with the strictest controls, we can never claim absolute certainty. Maybe coffee has this effect only on college students. Perhaps the coffee effect is negated by a particular study method. Would coffee have the same effect on a group of elementary students? Are there maximum and minimum levels after which there is no effect or a negative effect? Certainly, more research is needed in these areas.

Qualitative Research

As demonstrated above, quantitative research uses numbers to reach a state of knowing. Controlled environments are created to isolate one particular aspect of reality. The questions are stated up front and only data related to the research questions are observed and recorded. A cause-and-effect paradigm is used to make sense of the world.

Qualitative research, on the other hand, uses systematic observations to reach understanding. Researchers take the world as they find it instead of trying to manipulate conditions to isolate variables. The questions are more open ended and less defined, with plenty of room to collect a variety of data through collateral

TABLE 1.2   Results of Coffee on Achievement Test Scores

	PRETEST AVERAGE (%)	POSTTEST AVERAGE (%)	GAIN (%)
Treatment Group A	78	95	17
Control Group B	77	78	1

observations. Also, qualitative researchers sometimes begin a study with only a focus or area of interest and allow the specific research question to form or begin to be defined with early observations. To demonstrate the differences between quantitative and qualitative research, I include another mock study. This mock study also is purposely simplistic in order to highlight the salient elements of qualitative research.

The Coffee House Study.   When I went to college in the '70s, beer and bars were an integral part of the college culture, often the prime areas of socialization and interaction between genders. Many campuses even had a beer bar in their student union. Times have changed. The legal drinking age has gone up, awareness of the negative effects and dangerous situations created with the use of alcohol has increased, and most campuses today are alcohol free. This is something we could not have imagined in the '70s.

On the campus of Minnesota State University, where I work, coffee and coffee houses seem to have replaced beer and bars in the social milieu of the college culture. I wanted to see whether this was so. I was also interested in the nature of the interactions found in both types of environments.

Getting at my research questions meant going beyond numbers. I began my research spending a great deal of time observing the people and social interactions that took place in the coffee houses and bars found near our campus. I did not try to control or manipulate the environment; rather, I observed individuals within their natural environment. After several observations, I developed a systematic method for collecting data that initially included taking detailed field notes and interviewing students on campus and in the bars and coffee houses. (Data collection methods are described in detail in Chapter 8.) After my initial observations certain patterns of behaviors began to emerge. I created a checklist of these behaviors and put tally marks every time I saw them displayed. This checklist allowed me to quantify what I was seeing and provided me with a sense of the frequency, time, and gender related to each behavior.

In this study I became the lens through which this bit of reality was observed. My goal was to describe the quality of those things observed to help understand the nature of these places. What I found was that beer and bars were still an integral part of the social culture of this particular college campus. The types of interactions that occurred seemed similar in kind to what I remembered from the '70s. The music was loud and affrontive, the atmosphere was highly sexual, conversation tended to be short and light, groups that came together tended to splinter and mix, and there were many instances of initial intergender interaction (III); that is, boy meets girl or girl meets boy. A sort of mating dance was going on here, complete with colorful plumage, strutting, dancing, and establishing territory. All that was missing was two bucks charging at each other and locking horns. But I am sure, had I stayed longer, I would have observed this in some form.

In the coffee houses, the music tended to be quieter and more a part of the background. The general atmosphere seemed more subdued and cerebral without the sense of heightened sexuality. Also, conversation was on a much deeper level conceptually and of longer duration; groups very seldom splintered off or mixed with other groups; and initial intergender interactions rarely occurred.

It appeared as if beer and bars were still an integral part of college social interactions; however, because the age of legal alcohol consumption is 21 in Minnesota, most students found in the bars were in their junior and senior years. In this study I was not able to find out much about the socialization of younger students, but this is perhaps worthy of consideration for future research. It appears as if coffee and coffee houses have not replaced beer and bars in the college culture at Minnesota State University; rather, they have provided an additional outlet for a different kind of socialization.

Quantitative or Qualitative?

Is one type of research "better" than the other? No. Both are to be used to answer different kinds of questions. However, of these two categories of research, action research most often falls in the realm of qualitative research because action researchers study the world (their schools and classrooms) as they find them. And even though quantitative data may be collected, action researchers generally do not manipulate the environment to isolate variables. I often tell beginning action researchers to think of themselves as Jane Goodall studying a group of gorillas in the middle of the jungle.

TEACHING

Teachers and scientists are similar in many respects. Gallagher and Gallagher (1994) describe seven essential activities of a scientist. Each of these, in various forms, is also an essential part of teaching.

What Scientists and Teachers Do

1. *Scientists develop content expertise.* The process of science is highly dependent on having a well-organized knowledge base (Armbruster, 1993; Gallagher & Gallagher, 1994; Hodson, 1988; Thelen, 1984). Knowledge helps the scientist structure and assimilate new information. Scientific inquiries are built on accepted theories and previous research. New data make sense only when they are grounded in what is familiar. Thus, methods of science involve generating relations between prior knowledge and new knowledge (Johnson, 2000).

Effective teaching also requires knowledge related to subject matter, the learning process, and pedagogy. A sound knowledge base enables teachers to make thoughtful decisions about the teaching and learning process. Professional journals, workshops, conferences, and graduate courses are some traditional ways for teachers to expand their knowledge. Action research is one of the best ways to link theory to practice and expand teachers' knowledge base. (This is described in more detail in Chapter 3.)

2. *Scientists detect problems or ask questions.* As described above, scientists are continually asking questions about the universe and trying to solve problems (Stanovich, 1992). Teachers reflect on teaching experiences, looking for problems or ways in which to improve. They question and probe to see whether learning is occurring or whether students are grasping a particular skill or concept. The reflective teacher is continually asking, How is it going? How well and to what degree is learning taking place? What other strategies might I use? How is this new technique working?

3. *Scientists observe.* Scientists use observation in a variety of forms in collecting data. Kenneth Goodman (1986) tells us that effective teachers are kid-watchers. They watch their students as they work with new skills and concepts and listen to them as they engage in small-group discussions to see how learning is taking place and what skills need to be taught. Observation and reflection are skills that are used naturally by teachers as they monitor students engaged in the act of learning (Erickson, 1986).

4. *Scientists organize and classify data.* Scientists use forms of categorization such as phylum, classes, and divisions to put order to the natural world. Using authentic assessment techniques, teachers often record their observations using anecdotal records. These data are then organized by looking for patterns and put into context so that they can be used to inform instruction or to evaluate and report students' progress.

5. *Scientists measure or collect data.* Teachers measure and collect data when they give any form of standardized tests or use other forms of authentic assessment and evaluation. They monitor assignments, record scores, make anecdotal records, give standardized tests, and create checklists, all to help them answer the question, How well is learning taking place with my students? Measurement takes place as teachers determine how far students have progressed. Portfolios are used to show growth over time.

6. *Scientists hypothesize or make predictions.* Hypothesizing occurs also when teachers say, "I think this technique or this new teaching idea might work in my class." It also occurs when teachers try to understand a particular student or learning problem.

7. *Scientists experiment.* Experimenting occurs when teachers try a new technique or methodology, or implement a new solution to a problem.

SUMMARY

- Science is a body of knowledge generated by research.
- Science is also the process of asking and answering questions.
- Research is the systematic method used to collect data to answer questions.

- Quantitative or experimental research manipulates the environment to isolate a variable so that a cause–effect relationship can be determined.
- Qualitative research looks at the environment as it is and uses systematic methods to understand things happening there.
- Action research is a form of qualitative research.
- Teachers and scientists engage in many of the same kinds of activities.

QUESTIONS AND ACTIVITIES

1. What is your favorite branch of scientific inquiry?
2. What scientific inquiry or research influences your teaching?
3. Describe an instance in which you think beliefs are used to determine reality.
4. Describe one thing you believe to be true about teaching and learning (see Appendix A). Then describe the facts related to this belief.
5. Describe 3 to 10 facts about the act of teaching and about learning how to become a teacher. Then describe a belief related to teacher training (Appendix B).
6. Find a topic that interests you. It could be a topic related to education or something like humor, sewing, motorcycles, or football. Using a search engine on the Internet or on the database of a college library, plug in your topic followed by the word *research*. Find and describe a piece of research.
7. Pick one of the activities that scientists engage in as described by Gallagher and Gallagher (1994). Describe how this activity is manifest in your classroom or school.

RESEARCH PARADIGMS AND THE NATURE OF REALITY

The scientific knowledge that has been gained influences the way we perceive the world. But the way the world is experienced in a particular culture influences what kind of science gets developed by that society.

—Willis Harman, 1998, p. 28

This chapter examines how our metaphysical views and research perspectives influence our educational philosophy, which in turn affects educational practices.

METAPHYSICAL PERSPECTIVES

Willis Harman (1998) describes three views of reality that he calls metaphysical perspectives. *Metaphysical* here refers to ontology or the question of the origins of the universe and the nature of reality. These perspectives are materialistic monism, dualism, and transcendental monism. They determine the types of questions that get asked and answered and the types of data that are deemed valid in academic research.

Materialistic Monism

The materialistic monism perspective views the universe as being made up only of matter and energy. Consciousness is something that arises out of matter. That is, our sense of self is solely an end product of neurological activity, which in turn is an end product of millions of years of evolution. All things in this purely materialistic universe consist of the sum of their parts and can be understood by breaking them down into their most basic components and measuring that which is observed and experienced. Newtonian law of cause and effect governs all events and can be used to know, predict, and ultimately control all things.

Positivism, a philosophy consistent with this view, states that knowledge exists outside the individual. Truth can only be derived through objective observations that are proven through reliable tests and predictions (Alkove & McCarty, 1992). It is only by collecting empirical data, isolating variables, testing, and retesting that we obtain truth or say that a thing exists. Quantitative research methodologies are used to piece together small bits of knowledge in order to understand the world in which we live. The type of thinking valued here is deductive thinking or thinking in lines.

From this perspective, learning consists of receiving knowledge from outside the individual, which must then be demonstrated outwardly for it to have occurred. The purpose of schools is to supply students with a designated body of knowledge and skills in a predetermined order. Teaching is a matter of transmitting knowledge from point A (teacher's head) to point B (students' heads). Academic achievement is students' ability to demonstrate or retransmit this designated body of knowledge back to the teacher (point A) or some other measuring agency or entity. Quantitative psychometric methods are used exclusively to determine and describe intelligence.

Dualism

The dualistic perspective views the universe as comprising two distinctly different kinds of stuff: matter and energy, as well as consciousness. Here consciousness exists separately from matter. From this perspective, matter and energy are studied using the traditional tools of science described above. Consciousness (people's subjective interpretation of the outer phenomenal world) is studied using observations, descriptions, ethnographies, and interviews. Consciousness also pertains to the subjective interpretation of one's inner world of feelings, memories, and impressions. These are studied using interviews, gestalt, inner exploration, dream analysis, and art. Some will posit that consciousness also includes super-consciousness or spirituality.

Constructivism is an educational philosophy consistent with this view. Here, true knowledge is seen as personally constructed by individuals as they interact with the environment. Truth requires a value judgement and is different for each individual. We construct our truths by observing and combining events in the objective outer world with images and impressions occurring in the subjective inner world. Both quantitative and qualitative research methodologies are used here, but qualitative research using inductive thinking is more reflective of this metaphysical perspective. Inductive thinking can be thought of as thinking in circles. It is the process of inducing order on a field.

From this perspective, learning is an inner activity that uses both objective and subjective knowledge to constantly build and revise our cognitive webs. Learning then becomes a transaction between the learner and what is to be learned. The purpose of schools is to help students construct knowledge and develop the skills they will need to successfully live in their worlds. Teaching is a matter of creating conditions whereby students are able to transact with knowledge. Academic achievement is seen as students' ability to use their knowledge and skills to solve real-world problems or to create products or performances that are valued in one or more cultural settings. This reflects Howard Gardner's (1983) definition of intelligence. It also complements Robert Sternberg's (1996) concept of intelligence as using creative, analytical, and pragmatic thinking to adapt to or shape the world in which we live.

Transcendental Monism

Transcendental monism describes a universe in which the basic essence is consciousness. Here consciousness is primary, and matter and energy materialize from this. From this perspective ultimate reality is not found solely in the physical or phenomenal world as we know it; rather, it lies in a dimension or dimensions beyond the physical that is holomovement or the ground of all that there is (Talbot, 1991). Quantum physics describes such a reality in which all things in the physical universe are connected at the quantum level (Al-Khalili, 1999; Talbot, 1991). Physicist David Bohm said that the universe can be understood only if the unbroken wholeness is perceived in a way that does not reduce things to a series of individual entities (Nichol, 2003). At the quantum level, there is no fragmentation, only parts that are interconnected with greater systems and greater wholes. The things that we encounter in our phenomenal world (what Bohm calls "explicate reality") are merely an unfolding of a deeper reality ("implicate reality"), which is beyond our senses. It is consciousness, a very subtle form of energy, that creates movement from implicate order to the explicate order of our physical world (Bohm, 1980). Thus, consciousness is the cause and physical phenomena are the effect.

A helpful analogy can be found in music and the images created in the heads of listeners as they engage in the act of consciously attending to the music. The music can be thought of as holomovement or implicate reality. As the consciousness of the human listener interacts with the music, various mental images are created. These mental images, which do not exist in the absence of a conscious listener, are analogous to explicate reality. In this sense, phenomenal reality does not exist in the absence of an observer. This reflects the Copenhagen interpretation (Herbert, 1985), which posits that if a tree falls in a forest and nobody is there to hear it, not only does it not make a sound, but the tree does not exist in the first place.

Holism, a thesis consistent with this perspective, states that the universe is made up of integrated wholes that cannot be reduced to the sum of their parts. We can never come to know the whole of reality by isolating variables in order to examine small parts. Instead, the whole is best understood by examining the principles that govern behavior within the system. Both quantitative and qualitative methodologies are used here; however, they must always be combined with a greater perspective in the form of transcendental methodology in order to approach truth. Transcendental methodologies are those activities that allow an individual to move beyond personal consciousness (emotion, will, and logic) to approach universal consciousness and include: meditation, systematic contemplation, vision questing, the arts, journal writing, poetry and creative writing, personal narratives, stories, religious traditions, spirituality, sacred writing, deep silence, sensory deprivation, ritual, and chanting. These can all be used as a way of seeing and re-presenting reality. From this metaphysical perspective, all types of thinking are valued, although deep reflection, intuition, and associative thinking are used to provide the ultimate context.

Holistic education is based on theories of holism. It is constructed around the principle of interconnectedness and seeks to integrate multiple levels of meaning and experience (Miller, 1996). Making connections is central to the curriculum process here. These connections occur between concepts, subject areas, communities, cultures, humanity, the arts, the sciences, mythology, religion, ecological systems, and history. True knowledge is seen as ultimately residing within each individual. Thus, teachers strive to create experiences whereby students are able to encounter phenomena, both internal and external, so that this knowledge can be realized. To learn, one must transcend one's culture, bias, values, ego, past experience, and sense of self in order to see things as they really are. Learning is said to have occurred when this view elicits a transformation of consciousness that leads to a greater nurturing of self, others, and the environment. From this perspective, a school's fundamental purpose is the creation of better human beings, which occurs through self-actualization and self-transcendence (Maslow, 1971).

Intelligence here consists of two parts: the ability to perceive the whole and the ability to think and act in ways that nurture the self, others, and the environment. Intelligence, from this perspective, cannot be separated from these nurturing values. Classes are small and curriculums are flexible and multifaceted so that these students' particular talents can be easily displayed and nurtured. Teachers are then empowered and have the knowledge and skills to enable all students to develop their particular strengths; discover their passions; and engage in relevant, complex, real-world activities.

Three Perspectives in Perspective

Figure 2.1 provides a very general overview of how these metaphysical perspectives project into various areas. It is important to note that there are very few people who identify with or exist in only one column.

IMPLICATIONS

The purpose of this chapter is not to suggest that any one perspective should be adopted. Indeed, one of the current problems in education is that there is an over-reliance on materialistic monism and an overuse of quantitative research methodologies to define academic achievement and describe the quality of our learning experiences. Instead, I wish to make three points: First, we must recognize how our culture's predominant, some would say parochial, metaphysical perspective serves to shape the questions that get asked relative to education and educational

FIGURE 2.1
Metaphysical Perspectives

	MATERIALISTIC MONISM	DUALISM	TRANSCENDENTAL MONISM
1. worldview	universe consists of only matter and energy	universe consists of matter and energy, and mind-consciousness-spirit	the primary stuff of the universe is mind-consciousness-spirit
2. consciousness	consciousness arises from matter	exists separate from matter	matter arises from consciousness
3. reality	objective universe separate from observer	a personal construction	a dream
4. knowledge	*positivist:* exist outside self	*constructivist:* is constructed by individuals as they interact with the environment	*holistic:* exists within each individual, that which has the ability to transform
5. truth	objective examination of knowledge	requires a value judgment and is different for each individual	requires reflection and examination, an inward journey
6. learning	demonstrated outwardly for it to exist	inner state, constructing cognitive webs	free one's self from illusion, expand consciousness, transcendence
7. intelligence	ability to use linear thinking and deductive reasoning	ability to solve problems, create products, and shape environment	ability to perceive wholes and nurture self, others, and environment
8. purpose, teaching style	transmission	transaction	transformation
9. educational model	factory model	Dewey, social constructivist	Waldorf, Montessori, holistic education
10. primary psychological perspective	behaviorism	cognitive psychology	transpersonal psychology
11. primary research perspective	quantitative methodology	qualitative methodology	transcendental methodology
12. primary mode of thinking	deductive, lines	inductive, fields	intuitive, images, balls, B-cognition
13. scientific paradigm	phenonenological, cause–effect, natural laws, causal reality, atomistic, reductionist, positivistic	observational, objective, interpretive, contextual, subjective, ethnographic	quantum physics, holomovement, transcendentalism

practices. Recognizing this, the field of education needs to move toward a more expansive research agenda in terms of questions, methodology, and subject matter.

Second, we should reexamine and redefine the purpose of our schools. We do not ask the "why" questions often enough. It is our educational philosophies and assumptions about the nature of reality and the purpose of education that become the basis for our educational practice. I posit, as does Abraham Maslow (1971), that the fundamental purpose of education is self-actualization, which is to be fully human and to realize one's full potential. In this sense, our schools should be designed to help students identify and develop their abilities and discover their passions and interests. However, we cannot become fully human if we do not first recognize that which makes us so: our emotions, imagination, intuition, ideals, values, and creativity, none of which conveniently lend themselves to measurement. The Indian philosopher Jiddu Krishnamurti said, "The function of education is to create human beings who are integrated and therefore intelligent. . . . Intelligence is the capacity to perceive the essential, the what is; and to awaken this capacity, in oneself and in others, is education" (1953, p. 14).

Third, I am hoping that the three perspectives laid out in this chapter will move readers toward a broader conception of research. Again, research is a way of seeing and re-presenting reality. It runs the gamut from (a) strict, empirical, scientific experiments with controls used to isolate variables; to (b) descriptive, qualitative research; to (c) photography, the arts, poetry and creative writing, journal writing, and various forms of transcendental methodology. All of these can be used in action research projects to help you systematically observe your teaching practice with the goal of understanding and ultimately enhancing your ability to meet the various needs of your students.

SUMMARY

- Three primary metaphysical perspectives are materialistic monism, dualism, and transcendental monism.
- Our metaphysical perspectives influence educational research, which in turn affect our teaching practices.
- Materialistic monism suggests a universe that consists of only matter and energy. Knowledge exists outside the individual. Quantitative research methods align most closely with this perspective.
- Dualism suggests a universe that consists of matter and energy, and also mind, consciousness, and spirit. Knowledge is constructed by individuals as they interact with knowledge found in the environment. Qualitative research methods align most closely with this perspective.
- Transcendental monism suggests a universe that consists primarily of consciousness. True knowledge exists within each individual. Transcendental research methods align most closely with this perspective.

QUESTIONS AND ACTIVITIES

1. Which metaphysical perspective do you align with most closely? Within the perspective, which things do you disagree with?
2. How does your teaching philosophy align with your metaphysical perspective?
3. What do you perceive to be the purpose of our schools?
4. What are some important things relative to school, teaching, and learning that cannot be measured and quantified? How else might these things be expressed or represented?
5. If grades or standardized tests could not be used, how else might you describe a student's learning or growth?
6. Describe an instance in which intuition has served you well.
7. Find an interesting place. Use as many numbers as you can to describe that place quantitatively. Then, use words to describe that place qualitatively. Finally, use pictures, metaphors, poetry, or symbols to describe that place. What does the difference in your three descriptions tell you?

INTRODUCTION TO ACTION RESEARCH

Chapter 1 described research and the two major research categories. This chapter defines and describes action research and its various parts and examines the importance of action research in education.

RESEARCH IN ACTION

Action research can be defined as the process of studying a real school or classroom situation to understand and improve the quality of actions or instruction (Hensen, 1996; McTaggart, 1997; Schmuck, 1997). It is a systematic and orderly way for teachers to observe their practice or to explore a problem and a possible course of action (Dinkelman, 1997; McNiff, Lomax, & Whitehead, 1996). Action research is also a type of inquiry that is preplanned, organized, and can be shared with others (Foshy, 1998; Tomlinson, 1995).

A Quick Overview of Action Research

The action research process involves five essential steps or parts. First, ask a question, identify a problem, or define an area of exploration. Determine what it is you want to study. Second, decide what data should be collected, how they should be collected, and how often. Third, collect and analyze data. Fourth, describe how your findings can be used and applied. You create your plan for action based on your findings. And finally, report or share your findings and plan for action with others.

Action research is a recursive process that does not always proceed in a linear fashion (Patterson & Shannon, 1993). You may find yourself repeating some of these steps several times or doing them in a different order (see Figure 3.1). Also, some action research projects incorporate a sixth step, which is to put the findings or the question in a theoretical context called the literature review. This and the other steps are described in detail in the chapters that follow.

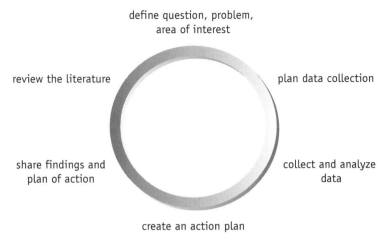

define question, problem,
area of interest

review the literature

plan data collection

share findings and
plan of action

collect and analyze
data

create an action plan

FIGURE 3.1   Steps of the Action Research Process

Descriptors of Action Research

The following nine descriptors may help bring this type of research into clearer focus.

1. *Action research is systematic.* Although data can be collected, analyzed, and presented with a certain amount of freedom, you must create a systematic way of looking. Action research is not a type of "anything goes" methodology. Nor is it a matter of simply describing what you think about an issue, depicting an interesting project or unit you have created, or explaining a pedagogical method that works well in your classroom. Action research is a planned, methodical observation related to one's teaching.

2. *You do not start with an answer.* An assumption underlying any research is that you do not know what you are going to find when you start; you are an unbiased observer. After all, if you had the answer, why would you be doing the research? Thus, even though you think Method X is the best way to teach reading, it is *not* appropriate to do a study describing why Method X is good and why Method Y is bad. Instead, you become an impartial observer (to the greatest degree possible) and study the effects of Method X as it is used in your classroom. The goal is to understand fully Method X and its effect (both positive and negative) on students' reading performance.

3. *An action research study does not have to be complicated or elaborate to be rigorous or effective.* Many beginning action researchers make the mistake of creating overly thick descriptions of every detail of their study in an attempt to be rigorous. This may often defeat the purpose. If too much material or too many details are included, you may miss what you are looking for and the report will probably not be read or understood. Thus, what you do not include is often just as important as what you do include in your observing and in your reporting. A well-organized, concisely described study is always preferable to a confusing, complicated study.

4. *You must plan your study adequately before you begin to collect data.* Having a plan and a schedule for collecting data before you start is what separates a systematic inquiry from an impressionistic view. However, plans and the type of data you collect can change as you get into your study.

5. *Action research projects vary in length.* The length of data collection in an action research study is determined by your question, the nature of your inquiry, the research environment, and the parameters of your data collection. For smaller action research projects I suggest that my graduate students who are classroom teachers consider 2 weeks as a minimum length. For undergraduate students, there are some very interesting sorts of projects that can be done in 1 or 2 class periods. Major studies, such as a master's thesis or an article for an academic journal, generally have a duration of 2 months to a whole school year. Keep in mind that if your data collection period is too short, you run the risk of presenting an unrealistic view of that educational setting.

6. *Observations should be regular, but they do not necessarily have to be long.* The duration of observations might be anywhere from 1 minute to an hour or more. Many of your observations might be a quick note with the date and time recorded, whereas others might be longer and more formal. Although they do not have to be long, observations do have to be done on a consistent, preplanned schedule. Also, observations are only one form of data collection. Other data collection forms and methods are described in Chapter 8.

7. *Action research projects exist on a continuum from simple and informal to detailed and very formal.* As stated above, some very interesting projects are short and simple. I suggest that beginning action researchers practice with these kinds of projects before tackling larger, more complicated ones. Action research can also be used for more formal kinds of studies. Many of my graduate students who are teachers have done action research projects for their master's theses. A sample guideline for this purpose is described in Chapter 15. Because these projects directly related to what was happening in their classrooms, these teachers were able to link theory to practice in a meaningful way. Graduate students have been far more enthusiastic about investing themselves in these kinds of projects than in the kinds of secondary research often done as part of a master's thesis. And not surprisingly, action research projects always seem to be more interesting and enjoyable to read.

8. *Action research is sometimes grounded in theory.* Relating the questions, results, and conclusions to existing theory provides a context in which to understand your research. Let the reader know how your data relate to what others have said about the same topic. Some action researchers do a short review of the literature before they begin collecting data, to provide a framework for the data collection. Others wait until the data are collected, then compare their conclusions to what others have written. Opinions as to the place and extent of a literature review in action research vary. This topic is discussed further in Chapter 7.

9. *Action research is not a quantitative study.* Many beginning action researchers have to divest themselves of their previous notions of the nature of research. In an action research project you are not trying to prove anything. You are not comparing one thing to another to determine the best possible thing. Also, there are no experimental or control groups, independent or dependent variables, or hypotheses to be supported. The goal is simply to understand. As an action researcher you are creating a series of snapshots in various forms and in various places to help us understand exactly what is going on.

To illustrate this concept of understanding, one night in a graduate class I asked a group of teachers to describe an event that happened that day. Alison Reynolds wrote of her interaction with a particular student that morning. Although she had described her teaching situation in early classes, it was not until I saw her snapshot of this student and the nature of their interactions that I began to understand some of the dynamics of her teaching situation. Her descriptions went far beyond the numbers and test scores in helping to comprehend the nature of teaching in an alternative high school and provided insight as to what an action research project might be. If she were to continue with this and make it an action project, she would create a plan for describing a number of students and situations in her school.

10. *The results of quantitative action research projects are limited.* While quantitative methods are sometimes used in action research, caution must be exercised in coming to generalized conclusions or in applying the results to larger populations. This is because of the small sample size of most action research projects and the many variables that are uncontrolled or unaccounted for.

For example, Mr. Miller did an action research project using quantitative methods to compare two approaches to reading instruction in his second-grade classroom. His statistical analysis found that the group using Method A scored significantly better than the group using Method B; however, Mr. Miller cannot reasonably conclude that Method A is the superior approach. The only conclusion he can reasonably make in this case is that Method A appears to be more effective than Method B. We do not know if the two groups were equal to begin with, we do not know if the samples were representative, it was conducted in an uncontrolled environment, and there was nothing to address the bias and subjectivity of the researcher. In order to make a stronger conclusion, each of these issues would need to be addressed.

In another example, Ms. Reuter wanted to see if her new approach to spelling instruction was effective in improving students' ability to spell words correctly. Using quantitative methods, she found that when using her new approach, students showed a statistically significant gain in their ability to spell words over the period of three months. However, like Mr. Miller she has to be very careful in the kinds of conclusions she can reasonably make. In this case, we do not know how much of this gain was a result of general learning and maturity. That is, students naturally become better spellers as they write and are exposed to more print. Also, she cannot reasonably compare her class to another class because of the differences in teaching styles and approaches as well as many other unaccounted variables. At best, she might be able to say that her new approach appears to be effective in helping students learn new words.

THE IMPORTANCE OF ACTION RESEARCH

This section describes how action research can be used to fill the gap between theory and practice in education, empower teachers to become agents of change, and enhance the professional growth and development of teachers.

The Gap between Theory and Practice

Among other things, research is used to build theories that in turn help determine the best practices in education. These practices are then used to help teachers create effective learning experiences. However, sometimes a gap exists between researchers conducting and reporting their education research and teachers practicing in the field (Hensen, 1996; Patterson & Shannon, 1993; Tomlinson, 1995). That is, what goes on in public schools often does not reflect the wealth of research related to best practice in teaching and learning.

There are two possible reasons for this gap: First, it may be because research in education is sometimes written in a way that does not respect the demands of teachers' daily schedules where time is a precious commodity. Research articles in academic journals can sometimes get overly descriptive, use jargon common to a very few, and focus on methodology and hypothetical notions that are not germane to the daily needs of teachers. This leads to the belief held by many teachers that education research is practically irrelevant (Barone, Berliner, Blanchard, Casanova, & McGown, 1996; Patterson & Shannon, 1993).

Second, the gap between research and practice might also be a result of the Moses Effect. This is when researchers hand down research edicts from on high with the expectation that teachers will be passive receivers of these edicts (see Figure 3.2). This creates a one-way flow of information that often does not value teachers' points of view, reflect the complexities of teaching, or address the concrete problems and concerns that teachers face in their classrooms on a daily basis (Patterson & Shannon, 1993).

Action research is one solution to use in bridging this gap (Hensen, 1996; Knight, Wiseman, & Cooner, 2000). The Action Research Quadrant (Figure 3.3) illustrates the two-way flow of information in action research. Theories and research related to best practice are used to understand and observe what is happening in a classroom setting. At the same time, this data is used to understand or inform theories and research related to best practice.

FIGURE 3.2   **The Moses Effect**

Teacher Empowerment

Action research also facilitates teacher empowerment. Teachers are empowered when they are able to collect their own data to use in making decisions about their schools and classrooms (Book, 1996; Erickson, 1986; Hensen, 1996). Empowered teachers are able to bring their talents, experiences, and creative ideas into the classroom, and implement programs and strategies that best meet the needs of their students. They also are able to use the methodologies that compliment their own particular philosophy and teaching style. When teachers are allowed to take risks and make changes related to teaching and learning, student achievement is enhanced (Marks, & Louis, 1997; Sweetland & Hoy, 2002) and schools become

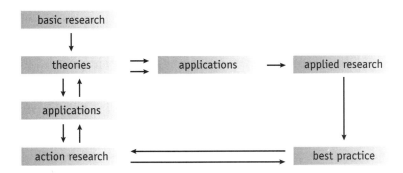

FIGURE 3.3   **The Action Research Quadrant**

more effective learning communities (Detert, Louis, & Schroeder, 2001). The top-down approaches that are sometimes used to manage schools and solve classroom problems create an external locus of control that inhibits teacher empowerment and thereby lessens the effectiveness of schools (Book, 1996).

Teacher Inservice and Professional Growth

Action research can also be used to replace teacher inservices as a means of professional growth and development. Traditional teacher inservices are often ineffective (Barone et al., 1996). Teachers are gathered, usually after a long day of teaching or on a busy workshop day, to listen to an expert describe an approach or methodology that often does not relate to their classroom situation or align with their teaching style. These traditional inservices generally do not give teachers sufficient time, activities, or content to increase their knowledge or affect their practice (Birman, Desimone, Porter, & Garet, 2000). To be effective, inservices need to be longer or extended over multiple sessions, contain active learning to allow teachers to manipulate the ideas and enhance their assimilation of the information, and align the concepts presented with the current curriculum, goals, or teaching concerns.

In regard to teachers' professional growth and development, Hensen (1996) describes the following benefits of action research: It (a) helps teachers develop new knowledge directly related to their classrooms, (b) promotes reflective teaching and thinking, (c) expands teachers' pedagogical repertoire, (d) puts teachers in charge of their craft, (e) reinforces the link between practice and student achievement, (f) fosters an openness toward new ideas and learning new things, and (g) gives teachers ownership of effective practices. Thus, providing teachers time and incentive to engage in action research projects and giving them a platform to present their findings and engage in professional dialogue with peers enhances their professional growth and development, which in turn moves the field of education forward. Using action research as a form of teacher development also increases the sense of professionalism in education (Tomlinson, 1995), and it enables teachers to become agents of change (Hensen, 1996). (Using action research for professional development is described further in Chapter 5.)

SUMMARY

- Action research is the process of studying a real school problem or situation.
- The goal of action research is to improve one's teaching practice or to enhance the functioning of a school.
- Action research is a preplanned and systematic observation of one's teaching practice or teaching situation.
- The essential steps of action research are to (a) define a question or area of study; (b) decide on a method for collecting data; (c) collect and analyze data; (d) describe how those findings can be used and applied; and (e) share your findings and plan for action with others.

- A review of the relevant literature related to your topic or question might also be included in action research.
- Action research can be used to bridge the gap between education research and teaching practice.
- Teacher empowerment can be facilitated with action research.
- Action research can be used as a replacement for traditional inservices to enhance teachers' professional growth and development.

QUESTIONS AND ACTIVITIES

1. List or describe three to five things that interest you in your classroom or school.
2. What are some problems in your classroom or school that you would like to solve?
3. What are some aspects of your teaching that you would like to improve?
4. Describe some theory or bit of research that seems to have no direct link to your teaching situation.
5. Describe some theory or bit of research that seems to have a direct link to your teaching situation.
6. Describe a situation where someone else has made a decision regarding your classroom practice. Would you have made the same decision?
7. Describe an instance where you would have made a different decision than what was made regarding your school or classroom. What reasons or evidence do you have to support your idea?
8. Think about the teacher inservices you have attended. What characteristics were effective? What characteristics were less effective? Use the T-chart in Appendix C to record your ideas.
9. What topic or topics would be of interest to you in a teacher inservice? Where might you go to get information on this topic?
10. Design a method that you think would be effective as a means for teacher growth and development.

USING ACTION RESEARCH FOR SOLVING PROBLEMS

Teachers are constantly challenged with a variety of problems for which they are required to develop solutions. Teachers who engage in action research projects become more flexible in their thinking, more receptive to new ideas, and thus better able to solve problems as they arise (Dinkelman, 1997). Problem solving consists of three elements: finding the problem, finding a solution, and testing the solutions. This chapter examines the use of action research in problem solving.

FINDING THE PROBLEM

Problems cannot be solved unless they are first identified and defined. Identifying the problem occurs when the situation is observed and there is a recognition that things could be done better. Defining the problem involves seeking to understand the nature of the situation and discovering the possible causal factors. You look to see why things are as they are. For example, why are students not learning? Why are behavior problems occurring on the playground? Why does Suzanne have problems getting her work in on time? Why has Steven been acting the way he has? As stated in previous chapters, action research can be used to help see what is happening in a school or classroom or to identify and define problems.

FINDING SOLUTIONS

A variety of strategies can be used to find a solution. Two are described next: creative problem solving and means–end analysis.

Creative Problem Solving

Creative problem solving (CPS) begins by defining the problem and generating ideas for solutions. The key to successful implementation of this strategy is to

FIGURE 4.1   Thinking Frame for CPS

1. Define the problem.
2. Generate as many solutions as possible.
3. Choose a solution that seems the best.
4. Elaborate and refine.
5. Implement the solution.
6. Review, evaluate, and refine as necessary.

produce as many ideas as you can. No evaluation of these initial ideas should be made as this would prevent the full range of possibilities from being explored. Sometimes when a new idea is put forth at a meeting or in a committee, individuals immediately respond by telling why that idea will not work. This only serves to preserve the status quo and prevent new and creative solutions from being considered. It is most effective to get all the ideas generated and listed, then engage in an evaluative discussion to choose the one that seems to be the best. Often two or three ideas can be combined for a solution. This would not be possible had you not first generated a number of ideas. The final steps are to refine, implement, and review and evaluate the solution. The CPS steps are listed in Figure 4.1.

Means–End Analysis

Means–end analysis (MEA) begins with a description of the desired outcome or end state. Where would you like to be? What outcome would you like to bring about? The next step is to define the goals necessary to bring about this end state. Goals are the global objectives, traits, skills, behaviors, or specific conditions of which your desired outcome is comprised. Goals are important in the eventual evaluation of your solution. That is, you can tell whether your solution is successful by ascertaining whether the goals are realized. Once the goals are described, the next step is to assess and describe the current situation. This is followed by an analysis of the means necessary to reach the end state. Finally, a plan is constructed to get from point A (current state) to point B (end state). And just like CPS, solutions need to be reviewed, evaluated, and refined after implementation. You may recognize that this problem-solving strategy is very similar to the process used in designing new curricula. The MEA steps are listed in Figure 4.2.

Problem-Solving Strategies in the Classroom

We cannot assume that students know how to solve problems effectively unless they first have been taught how to do so. The two problem-solving strategies just described can be taught to students in the form of thinking skills. This will improve their ability to solve problems and also enhance learning (Johnson, 2000). I recom-

FIGURE 4.2   Thinking Frame for MEA

1. Describe the desired outcome.
2. Define the goals necessary to reach the end state.
3. Describe the current state.
4. Analyze the means necessary to get the desired outcome.
5. Construct and implement a plan.
6. Review, evaluate, and refine the plan.

mend starting with CPS as this is usually easiest for most students. You may want to simplify some of the steps for younger students.

You can teach problem-solving strategies in six steps. First, use the thinking frames in Figures 4.1 and 4.2 to create a poster to display in the classroom as a teaching aid. A thinking frame is a concrete representation of a particular cognitive process broken down into specific steps and used to support the thought process (Johnson, 2000; Perkins, 1987). Second, identify the problem-solving strategy and describe each step. Third, model the problem-solving strategy by thinking out loud as you go through the steps to solve a problem. Fourth, use guided practice to solve a problem together. Fifth, create problems for students to solve by themselves or in small groups. And finally, embed problems into all aspects of the curriculum. For example, in reading or literature use problems found within stories for students to solve. These can be interpersonal problems, problems that need the invention of a new product or process, or organizational problems. For social studies, science, and math, use problems that are found in history, society, or real life.

TESTING THE SOLUTION

The final part of problem solving is to implement the solution and test it to see whether it works. Every new plan, program, or solution needs some adjusting during the implementation stage. Action research can be used as formative and summative evaluation. The next section is a description of how I used action research along with the three elements of problem solving to improve my teaching practice.

AN EXAMPLE OF ACTION RESEARCH AND PROBLEM SOLVING

I used to be the gifted education specialist for an elementary school in rural Wisconsin. In my first year in this position I conducted pullout sessions in which I met with small groups of students once a week. (This was several years ago. I would not recommend this as the most effective strategy today.) My students used to love the chance to learn more complex subjects, engage in high-level thinking, and have discussions and debates with like-minded peers. During my third year in the district, my job expanded and I took over the gifted education duties in the middle and high school. I was excited to resume weekly pullout sessions with a group of middle school students with whom I had not worked since my first year. However, at our first pullout session I found that my formerly eager and excited students were sullen and distant. They sat at the back of the room and rarely spoke or contributed, and when they did, it was with little enthusiasm.

Finding the Problem

A bit of problem finding and defining was needed. Had I tried to address this problem without first trying to understand the situation, I would have missed the whole point and probably made the situation worse. Instead, I gathered data by creating a systematic plan whereby I talked with students individually, talked with their teachers, and observed these students in a variety of classroom situations. I also went back and reread my textbooks on human development. What I discovered was that these young adolescents were reacting negatively to being singled out from their peers. They did not want to be apart from the group or be thought of as somehow different, which was a very normal reaction for students at this developmental stage.

Finding a Solution

Having identified and defined the problem, the next step was to find a solution. I used MEA. The desired outcome was to create meaningful and enriching learning experiences whereby these students could reach their full potential. The goals were to engage these students in enriched content, teach high-level skills, and give them choices so that they could pursue topics of interest to them. The current state comprised three elements: (a) these students were engaged in a classroom curriculum that was far below their capabilities; (b) my pullout sessions were unrelated to their regular curriculum; and (c) a certain amount of social stress was being caused by separating these students from their peers.

It was clear that I had to create a structure that allowed these students to solve problems and create plans or products within their regular classroom experience. The gifted education literature describes a strategy called compacting and differentiation whereby students are able to test out of a unit to free up time to do other projects (Renzulli & Reis, 1997). The advantage of this approach is that it can be made available to all students and thus bypass the need for the formal identification of gifted students. It also reflects Howard Gardner's definition of intelligence, which is the ability to solve problems or create products that are valued within one or more cultural settings (1983).

To implement this plan I worked with classroom teachers to design a structure that allowed students who had met a criterion pretest score to engage in inquiry projects, individually or in small groups, that were related to the curriculum. Contracts were used to define specific goals, steps, and time lines to be met (see Figure 4.3). Instead of conducting weekly pullout sessions, I was in charge of a resource center where students would come to work on their independent projects (see Appendix D). Among other things, I worked with students to teach them the skills necessary to complete their projects.

FIGURE 4.3   Contracts for Inquiry Projects

Plan to Investigate

Investigator: _____

BEFORE THE INVESTIGATION

1. What is your question? What are you curious about? What do you want to investigate?

2. Important background knowledge? Use at least two sources to get information about your question. You may want to interview experts, read books or magazines, or use the Internet.

3. How will you collect data?

read ____	observe ____	checklist ____
weigh ____	measure ____	survey ____
interview ____	time ____	create and test ____
listen ____	count ____	other ____

4. When will you present your findings to the class?

AFTER THE INVESTIGATION

5. Organize your data. (Look for groups or patterns, put it in order, or use tables or graphs.)

6. What conclusions can you make or what interesting ideas do you have based on your data?

7. How will you present your data and conclusions or ideas?

lab report ____	video ____	poster ____
photos ____	plan ____	visual art ____
graph ____	story ____	demonstration ____
brochure ____	speech ____	other ____

In looking at Figure 4.3, note that the inquiry projects contain the same elements as a teacher action research project. The research process I am describing in this book can be used and adapted to design inquiry activities for students at all grade levels.

Testing the Solution

Once this structure was in place (it took about 2 months to get it up and running), I designed a systematic plan for collecting data to evaluate the effectiveness of this program. I used student and teacher surveys, recorded field notes related to my work in the resource center, and analyzed students' projects. Essentially, I was using action research as a form of program evaluation. This collection and analysis of data helped me to revise and refine this program. Some of my findings included the following: (a) I worked with more students than just those who were formally identified; (b) many students who were not formally identified as gifted created projects that were just as outstanding as those who were formally identified; (c) students enjoyed having choice as well as challenge; and (d) teachers enjoyed having a gifted education strategy that augmented the regular curriculum.

SUMMARY

- Solving problems is an inherent part of teaching.
- Problem solving consists of three parts: finding the problem, finding a solution, and testing the solutions.
- Creative problem solving and means–end analysis are two strategies that can be used to solve problems.
- Problem-solving strategies can be taught to students to improve their ability to solve problems.
- Problem solving can be embedded within a curriculum to enhance learning and reinforce problem-solving strategies.
- Action research can be used to identify and define problems and to evaluate solutions.

QUESTIONS AND ACTIVITIES

1. Find a picture book or a chapter in a trade book that you might use with students. Generate a list of problems associated with each.
2. List five to ten real-life problems related to science or society. Describe where and how these might be integrated into a curriculum.

3. Find a problem related to your daily life in some way. This could be an interpersonal problem, or a problem related to school, work, or some product or process. Use CPS (Appendix E) to generate ideas and find a solution.
4. Find a problem specifically related to education. Use MEA machine (Appendix F) to design a plan.
5. Find a problem in your classroom or personal life situation, then define it. Why is it occurring?
6. Find a solution in your classroom or personal life. How might you evaluate that solution?

STRATEGIES FOR PROFESSIONAL GROWTH: PRESERVICE AND INSERVICE TEACHERS

PRESERVICE TEACHERS: A TOOL FOR SEEING

Preservice teachers have a great deal of information to assimilate in making the transition from student to beginning teacher. Teaching is a very complex endeavor. It is easy for veteran teachers to forget what it is like to try to begin to understand subject area knowledge, learning theory, classroom management, and pedagogical methods, and at the same time to try to comprehend student interactions and the subtle nuances of the classroom environment. Experienced teachers have a large knowledge base related to each of these that is used to perceive and quickly process information. However, the knowledge base of preservice teachers is often shallow and disjointed and, thus, processing new information and making decisions takes more time. Action research can add to this knowledge base by helping preservice teachers see things in the classroom they may not have previously noticed. This process speeds up their assimilation of information and enables them to make better decisions more quickly.

One word of warning along these lines for teacher educators: Make sure you do not overwhelm preservice teachers in using action research. Observations should be done only during those times when they are not responsible for teaching. Also, keep action research projects short and focused. It is much more beneficial for a preservice teacher's growth and development to try to understand one thing thoroughly rather than many things partially.

Three types of observations can be used with preservice teachers: observing students, observing classroom teachers, and observing their own practice.

Observing Students

1. *Map student movement.* Create a map of the classroom. During a work time or a less structured time, pick two or three students to observe. Use different colored markers to chart the movement of each student.

2. *Observe and compare students of varying abilities.* Find a student who seems to have a great deal of success in the classroom and another who often seems to experience failure. Use the T-chart in Figure 5.1 to record the verbal and nonverbal behaviors of each. What might this tell you about what each experiences on a daily basis?

3. *Observe and compare students in different environments.* Select a student who seems not to have a great deal of success in the classroom. Use the T-chart in Figure 5.2 to see how the behaviors of this student might change at recess, an environment in which failure is not a predominant component.

4. *Observe the playground.* Watching students in the less structured environment of the playground can provide a good sense of their developmental levels, both socially and emotionally. Use a notebook and observe at least two recess periods. You might choose to observe one of the following conditions: the games played, the groups that form, interaction patterns, the type of humor observed, the organization of the games, the number and types of interactions, or gender patterns. You might also observe the social dynamics. Who appear to be the leaders? Why? What do these leaders do to assert their leadership?

5. *Observe the length of time on a particular task.* Observe one or two students as they are engaged in an academic task such as writing, reading, or doing homework. How long are they able to stay on task? How much time is allotted to various tasks each day? Observe several students over the course of a week and create a graph the shows your results.

6. *Observe behavior and speculate as to the motivation.* The T-chart in Figure 5.3 can be used to note interesting or unusual student behavior, either in the classroom or at recess. This T-chart is a common tool used by social and other scientists and can be used in a variety of situations (see Appendix C). Observations are recorded in

FIGURE 5.1 T-Chart for Observing Students

MORE SUCCESSFUL STUDENT	LESS SUCCESSFUL STUDENT

Conclusions, observations, or ideas:

FIGURE 5.2   T-Chart for Observing Environments

CLASSROOM	RECESS

Conclusions, observations, or ideas:

the left column. Recorded on the right is your analysis or your thoughts related to each observation. For action research projects, record behaviors in the column on the left and in the column on the right, speculate as to motivation or why you think the student or students acted as they did. For example, what did they hope to gain or achieve? What prompted or precipitated the behavior? (You may need to conduct interviews.)

7. *Record writing topics.* Make a list of those things students write about when they are given their choice of topics. Look for groups. What does this tell you about what is important in the lives of these students?

FIGURE 5.3   T-Chart for Observing Behaviors and Possible Motivation

BEHAVIOR OBSERVED	YOUR ANALYSIS

Conclusions, observations, or ideas:

Observing Classroom Teachers

One of the best ways for preservice teachers to begin to develop their own teaching style is to observe other teachers. You can usually find one teacher who seems to be a mentor or who might be used as a model for your own teaching style. As time goes on, you will find yourself collecting bits and pieces from all the teachers you encounter.

This section is not meant to be used as a tool to critique teachers. Instead, the following activities are designed to help you find those teacher traits and strategies that might be incorporated into your own teaching style. Notice and record the following:

1. *Management techniques.* Use a notebook to record teacher behaviors related to classroom management. What kinds of management systems and strategies does this teacher employ? Notice instances in which the teacher acted in a proactive manner to avoid behavior problems.
2. *Questions and responses.* Observe a classroom to see what kinds of questions are asked. Record the questions and student responses.
3. *Levels of questions.* Use the chart in Figure 5.4 to determine the level of questions as described by Bloom's Taxonomy.
4. *Strategies for engaging students.* Record the strategies the teacher uses to get students' attention or to keep them engaged. Look for interesting activities or effective techniques that you might try.
5. *Interesting observations and your analysis.* Use a T-chart to record interesting or important observations during the day, and also your analysis of those observations (see Figure 5.3).
6. *Assessment and evaluation.* Use a tally mark to indicate the type of assessment and evaluation the teacher uses to observe learning each day (see Figure 5.5).

FIGURE 5.4   Taxonomical Level of Questions

Use a tally mark to indicate level of questions asked.

Knowledge	
Comprehension	
Application	
Analysis	
Synthesis	
Evaluation	

FIGURE 5.5   Types of Assessment and Evaluation

Standardized test	
Criterion-based test	
Portfolio assessment	
Checklists	
Rubric	
Homework	
Informal assessment	

Observing Your Own Practice

The word *practice* should be stressed in the heading above. What you are doing as a preservice teacher is practice. It is expected that you will make mistakes. If you have never made a mistake, you have not tried enough things. Teachers of all levels of experience and mastery make mistakes. What separates the average teacher from the master teacher is that the master teacher engages in critical reflection to determine what can be changed the next time. Knowing this, hopefully you can eliminate some of the anxiety you may feel.

I encourage the preservice teachers that I work with to use audiotape occasionally to record their teaching episodes. I prefer this to videotape as it is much easier and far less intrusive to use. It is easy to turn on a tape recorder, set it on the front table, and begin teaching. It is more difficult to set up a camera, adjust the view, and acclimate students to it. Except for student movement and certain nonverbal behaviors, just as much information is collected with audiotape.

1. *Types of questions.* Use tally marks to indicate the number of times a particular type of question was asked (see Figure 5.6).
2. *Level of questions.* Using Bloom's Taxonomy as a conceptual model, determine the level of most of your questions. You can display this information in graph form (Figure 5.4).

FIGURE 5.6   Types of Questions

Open-ended questions	
Closed-response questions	

FIGURE 5.7   Management Statements

Proactive management statements	
Reactive management statements	

3. *Wait time.* Use a stopwatch to determine the length of time between when you ask a question and when you call on a student. Record these times. Use a bar graph to show the number of times at each interval level, or use a line graph to show how the time interval changed over the duration of the class.
4. *Management statements.* Figure 5.7 can be used to record the types of statements made related to classroom management. A proactive management statement is one that is used to avoid a situation. A reactive management statement is one that is a reaction to something that has already happened.
5. *Observation and analysis.* Use the T-chart (Appendix C) to record interesting or important parts of your lesson and your analysis of those parts.

PROFESSIONAL DEVELOPMENT SCHOOLS

For all the talk of educational reform, there have been relatively few major restructuring efforts in teacher education programs (Imag & Switzer, 1996). Typical teacher education programs consist of a collection of education courses, a few short practicum field experiences, and student teaching (McIntyre, Byrd, & Foxx, 1996). Some of the problems with this approach include the following:

1. *Traditional teacher preparation programs often ignore the shallow and disjointed nature of preservice teachers' knowledge as it relates to teaching and learning.* The importance of knowledge in all areas has been well documented. Bereiter and Scardamalia (1992) explain that background knowledge is used to lessen the cognitive demands of problem solving, to guide perception, and to organize and encode new information. Research has shown that knowledge positively affects perception (Chase & Simon, 1973), categorization and problem solving (Chi, Feltovich, & Glaser, 1981; de Groot, 1965), general learning (Bereiter & Scardamalia, 1992; Glaser, 1984), reading comprehension (Goodman, 1986; Smith, 1985), and memory (Recht & Leslie, 1988). However, most preservice teachers have spent very little time in a classroom and, as a result, their experiential knowledge base related to teaching and learning is limited. This makes it very difficult to place new skills and concepts in a meaningful context or see the application of theory. Thus, transference of learning from the college classroom to teaching situations is slight.

2. *Skills and concepts are learned in isolation instead of in context.* Skills in teaching cannot be taught as a series of subskills (Eisner, 1983). Learning of any kind pro-

ceeds best from whole-to-part-to-whole (Gambrell & Mazzoni, 1999). In education this means that preservice teachers should first be immersed in an authentic teaching experience (whole) in order to provide a context to see how and where skills and concepts are applied. Next, these skills and concepts (parts) should be taught while preservice teachers are immersed in that experience. Finally, preservice teachers should be engaged in student teaching experiences (whole) to practice skills and concepts already learned.

3. *Field experiences before student teaching tend to be short and disjointed.* Short drive-by experiences of three weeks or less do not allow preservice teachers to develop relationships with students, to see change occurring over time, or to get an accurate sense of the dynamic nature of teaching as it unfolds throughout the day. Instead, they are left to figure out how all the parts are connected to the whole of teaching (McIntyre et al., 1996).

4. *True collaboration or partnerships between universities and public schools do not exist.* These relationships are an integral part of teacher preparation programs; however, they have generally been directed by the university (Book, 1996). Teachers' roles tend to be limited to meeting the needs of the university. The resulting one-way flow of communication puts teachers in a subservient role and limits their contribution. In a true partnership, communication and information flow two ways. Although universities must always have the final say in preparing teachers (we are the ones, after all, who are visited by accrediting agencies), a more equitable university–school partnership allows greater teacher input and enhances the overall quality of teacher preparation.

5. *University professors have few opportunities to model the latest teaching methods.* University professors become more credible when they are able to experiment, try new methodologies, and model pedagogy for preservice and classroom teachers (Book, 1996). This modeling is also an effective way to add new teaching techniques to the repertoire of classroom teachers.

6. *Classroom teachers have few opportunities to share their teaching knowledge and expertise.* Experienced teachers have insight related to the everyday practice of teaching; however, they are often not able to share the wealth of their accumulated knowledge unless student teachers are assigned to their room. But even in this situation the preservice teacher hears only one teacher's perspective. Preservice teachers benefit from hearing a broad range of ideas from experienced teachers.

7. *A cohesive structure often is missing from methods courses and practicum field experiences.* Many teacher education programs lack a unifying force (McIntyre et al., 1996). A series of unrelated practicum field experiences does not serve to create a unifying structure. Preservice teachers learn more when field experiences are organized and clearly articulated (Metcalf, Hammer, & Kahlich, 1996). Thus, practicum field experiences should correspond to a set of goals established for the entire teacher education program (Guyton & McIntyre, 1990).

A New Approach to Teacher Preparation

The professional development school (PDS) is a new approach to teacher growth and development. Here, a school and university work together to create a new kind of learning community. Undergraduate education courses are taught on site at a school. Preservice teachers spend part of their day assisting classroom teachers in daily instruction, teaching in small groups, and doing some whole-class instruction.

The hallmark of the professional development school is a true partnership between a school and a university. Thus, classroom teachers are used to instruct parts of undergraduate methods courses and, at the same time, university instructors are able to teach models of the latest pedagogical techniques in a classroom setting. Some of the advantages of the professional development school are that it (a) allows master teachers to share their knowledge and experience, (b) facilitates the infusion of new ideas into a school, (c) provides teaching assistance for the classroom teacher, and (d) allows preservice teachers to be immersed in an authentic teaching context and thereby to see how theory is interpreted in practice.

Action research is an integral part of the professional development school. Preservice teachers use the ideas described above to begin to see the many facets of classroom teaching. Also, the collaborative nature of the PDS allows classroom teachers and university instructors to collaborate in order to study questions that are of interest to both. Action research is conducted in this setting to improve teaching practice, to understand issues related to school life, and to enhance the quality of the school. This type of research is essential for the continued growth of our field. It is only through the discovery and dissemination of new ideas that we can continue to shape education and move it forward. This is essential if we are to keep pace with the rapid changes occurring at all levels of society. Action research allows the voice and perspectives of the classroom teacher to be part of this evolution.

ACTION RESEARCH AND THE PROFESSIONAL DEVELOPMENT OF TEACHERS

Professional development continues long after one leaves a college or university and thus is a task that must be shared by public schools and teacher preparatory institutions. Action research is perhaps the most efficient and effective way to address the professional development of teachers. As stated at the beginning of this book, action research allows teachers to connect education theory and research to their classroom practice and helps them to become more reflective and analytical in their teaching practice. Action research is also very economical in terms of the time and money invested and the returns garnered in the form of increased learning by students and improved practice by teachers.

I would encourage school districts and universities to begin to work together and to begin to think in new ways about graduate education, learning, and professional development. We must dispel the notion that learning takes place only when a professor stands in front of a group of teachers and tells them things. One idea to consider, and one that we have used in the Department of Educational Studies: Special Population at Minnesota State University, Mankato, is to recognize and grant credit for teacher action research projects with accompanying presentations. This creates learning that is more specific to each teacher's classroom situation and also serves to improve the professional status of teachers.

SUMMARY

- A knowledge base related to subject areas, learning theory, classroom management, and pedagogical methods is important in teaching and learning to teach.
- Preservice teachers often have shallow and disjointed knowledge bases related to the various parts of teaching, and thus processing new information related to these areas is difficult.
- Action research can be used to help preservice teachers recognize many of the important elements of teaching in an authentic context and thereby improve their ability to assimilate the many facets of teaching.
- Preservice teachers benefit from observing students, classroom teachers, and their own teaching practice.
- The professional development school, of which action research is an integral part, is a new approach to teacher preparation whereby schools and universities work together to form learning communities.
- Action research is an efficient and effective method of attending to the professional development of teachers.

QUESTIONS AND ACTIVITIES

1. Describe the knowledge you think is important for teaching. What do teachers need to know or know about?
2. What skills are important for teaching? What do teachers need to be able to do?
3. Describe your philosophy of learning. How do students learn?
4. Practice using one of the techniques described in this chapter. Share your results and any insights you have about the process.
5. What do you think is the best way to prepare preservice teachers for the rigors of classroom life?
6. What do you think is the best way for classroom teachers to continue their professional growth and development?

THE PROCESS

THE BEGINNING

"But how do I start for Emerald City?" Dorothy asked. Glinda replied, "It's always best to start at the beginning. And all you do is follow the Yellow Brick Road."

—*The Wizard of Oz*, 1939

AN OVERVIEW OF THE ACTION RESEARCH PROCESS

Chapter 3 described five essential parts of action research. In this chapter, these five parts are broken down further into nine steps. These steps are meant to be a guideline to be adapted to your particular research topic or situation. Also, as stated previously, there is no universal order to these steps. You might find yourself skipping steps, rearranging their order, or repeating some steps more than once.

Action Research Steps

1. *Identify a problem or research topic.* The first step is to decide what to study. What are you curious about? What piques your interest? Ask a question, identify a problem, or define an area of interest for exploration. Find something that intrigues you, something you would really like to examine in depth.

2. *Set the problem or research topic in a theoretical context.* This means doing a review of the literature. (This is described in detail in Chapter 7 and Chapter 16.) Look in professional journals, books, and web sources to see what others have found out or have to say about your research topic. Relating your research topic to current theories gives you more credibility and provides a theoretical context for your findings. Also, this enables you to link theory and practice by connecting what you find in the literature to what is happening in your classroom.

You might take one of three approaches in doing a literature review. The first approach is to do the review of the literature before you begin collecting data. Besides setting your study in a theoretical context, the literature might also be used to help formulate your question, refine a pedagogical method to be studied, or give you ideas for collecting data. The second approach is to review the literature as you report the data and make your conclusions. The literature is related to each of your concluding points. The third approach is not to do a review of the literature at all. Many short action research projects do not include this element.

As you can see, you have a certain amount of freedom in organizing your action research project. The onus is on you, however, to create a credible and coherent report. Linking your study to theories and previous research is one way to do this.

3. *Make a plan for data collection.* In traditional research this is known as methodology. What data are you going to study? How are you going to collect the data? How often will you collect data? Action research is not impressionistic. Nor is it a brochure supporting a particular teaching methodology. Rather, action research is a systematic observation; therefore, data collection must be focused and the elements of data collection must be determined *before* the research begins.

4. *Begin to collect and analyze data.* After you have identified at least two kinds of data, you begin the data collection process. As you collect your data, analyze them by looking for themes, categories, or patterns that emerge. This analysis will influence further data collection by helping you to know what to look for.

5. *If necessary, allow the question or problem to change as you collect data.* Action research is a dynamic, ever-changing process. As a human you cannot help but be influenced by the data you collect. It is very common, therefore, to change a particular teaching strategy, the sources of data, or even the focus of the study as you are collecting data. This is acceptable as long as you let the reader know what you did and why you did it. That is, in writing your report take the reader along with you in all phases of your action research.

6. *Analyze and organize the data.* Hopefully you have been analyzing and organizing the data as you have been collecting them, thus, step 6 should be the final step of an ongoing process. In analyzing your data you need to establish how many total things were recorded, how many categories or kinds of things there are, and how many things are in each category. This is a quick view of analytic induction, which is described in Chapter 9.

7. *Report the data.* Present the facts or findings. This presentation includes an overview with detailed descriptions and illustrative samples of important events, activities, and responses. Also reported are the number and types of themes, categories, or patterns present in the data. In this section of your report you take the role of a journalist or anthropologist by describing what you saw and providing examples that demonstrate your perceptions.

8. *Make your conclusions and recommendations.* The next step is to interpret the data or tell the reader what they mean. Based on the data, what can you conclude? What do you recommend based on your conclusions? You then answer your research question, provide answers for a problem, or make suggestions based on your new understanding. Also, as stated in step 2, some action researchers do a review of the literature at this point to set their conclusions in a theoretical context.

9. *Create a plan of action.* This is where you put the action in action research. Based on your conclusions and recommendations, what will you do? You create a plan of action. And as you implement your plan of action, you assess what is happening or how effective it is; thus, the action research cycle continues.

FINDING YOUR RESEARCH TOPIC

To begin you must first determine an area to research. Three common research possibilities include the following: (a) study or evaluate a teaching method, (b) identify and investigate a problem, or (c) examine an area of interest.

A Method

Would you like to try a new teaching method or technique? Maybe you want to see how a writing workshop works. Perhaps you are interested in finding out what happens if you let students choose their own writing topics. What new method or teaching idea might you be willing to experiment with in your classroom?

Chris Reed, a primary grade teacher, was intrigued by the idea of using an embedded approach to spelling. Instead of the prescribed list of spelling words and traditional approaches to spelling instruction, she used words found in students' literature and science units and created her own activities. Some weeks she also experimented with allowing students to choose their own words to study. She wanted to see whether this approach was effective in improving students' ability to spell under real writing conditions. As she started her action research project, she also became interested in seeing whether this approach was more enjoyable for her students, what effects it might have on students' writing, what kind of words students chose to study, and how these words related to the lives of students.

Mary Kaymeyer, a fifth-grade teacher, had always loved teaching her poetry unit in language arts, but, because of a crowded curriculum, she felt she never had enough time to really enjoy and explore this form as much as she would like. She decided try embedding poetry across her fifth-grade curriculum. Mary redesigned her curriculum so that poetry was included in social studies, math, science, health, and reading as well as in language arts classes. Poetry was used to reinforce important concepts and to create alternatives to tests and written reports in helping students organize and demonstrate their knowledge. After her first year of using this approach, she decided to use action research to see how it was going and to provide support for either continuing or abandoning this idea.

Identifying a Problem

Do you think a subject or an area in your teaching does not flow as well as others? Do you think a particular problem in your school or classroom is disrupting the learning process? Action research is a tool that can be used to systematically study a problem area. It can be used to understand what is happening and the possible causes of the problem. It can be used to explore various solutions. Also, a review of the literature can be used to help connect the literature to the problem and to find solutions that others may have tried.

Al Norton, a high school social studies teacher, noticed that the students in his senior-level classes seemed to be bored and disinterested. They appeared to be going through the motions on weekly assignments and often were talking or zoning out during class. He conducted a series of short written surveys and class discussions to find out what students were interested in, what they wanted to learn, how they best liked to learn, and what was useful in helping them understand new ideas. This allowed Al to connect his social studies curriculum to issues that were relevant to students. A review of the literature gave him ideas for using different teaching strategies and activities. Al also shared his findings with his students and, in so doing, modeled a method of inquiry used by social scientists.

Examining an Area of Interest

Are you interested in a particular topic? Are you curious about something? Action research can be used to explore your interests. For example, Jim Soderholm, a middle school English teacher, has always been interested in comedy and humor. He wanted to discover what middle school students found funny and how they used humor in their socialization process. He began his study by recording instances of students' humor that he observed in classes, in the halls, or in other situations. From this, he created a form that allowed him quickly to note the instance of humor, the name and gender of the humorist, the recipient of the humor, and the type of humor (see Figure 6.1).

FIGURE 6.1   Form for Recording Students' Humor

Date:	Time:	Place/setting:
Name of humorist:		Gender:
Humor recipient:		
Type of humor:		

Key for humor recipient: 1 = student to student; 2 = student to teacher; 3 = student to anybody

Key for type of humor: P = physical humor; S = sarcastic; A = absurd or silly; W = word play; S = sexual

This project improved Jim's teaching in three ways. First, it helped him further his understanding of his students and the nature of their social interactions and emotional status. Second, he found humor to be a hot topic for these middle school students. This led him to incorporate humor into his English curriculum by teaching students to write and perform their own stand-up routines and comedy sketches. Third, Jim shared the findings of his action research with his students. They were fascinated by what he discovered and the process he used. This led to him teaching students how to do their own inquiry projects. Jim was able to use their accompanying reports as vehicles for teaching technical writing skills, oral speaking, and presentation techniques.

SUMMARY

- The five parts of action research described in Chapter 3 can be broken down further into nine steps: (a) identify a problem or research topic; (b) set the problem or research topic in a theoretical context; (c) make a plan for data collection; (d) begin to collect and analyze data; (e) allow the question or problem to change as you collect data; (f) analyze and organize the data; (g) report the data; (h) make your conclusions and recommendations; and (i) create a plan of action.
- The order and nature of these nine steps should be adapted to suit the demands of one's research topic and teaching situation.
- Finding a topic or an area of interest is one of the beginning steps of an action research project.
- Three research possibilities are to examine a teaching method, a problem, or an area of interest.

QUESTIONS AND ACTIVITIES

1. Describe the new teaching methods or ideas you would like to try.
2. Generate a list of problems or areas that might be improved in your school or classroom.
3. Describe your interests related to teaching, learning, or human interaction.

A THEORETICAL CONTEXT

This chapter contains a brief description of a literature review and how it might be used in an action research project. More specific instructions on how to create a literature review are described in Chapter 16.

REVIEWING THE LITERATURE

A literature review is an examination of journal articles, ERIC documents, books, and other sources related to your action research topic. The purpose of the review is to set your topic in a theoretical context and to make a connection between theory and your classroom practice.

A literature review also helps tie your action research project to what others have said and done before you. That is, you do not have to reinvent the wheel; instead, you can use the insights of others to make your research more efficient and effective. A review of the literature may also provide you with examples of classroom applications, research questions, data collection methods, or data analysis techniques.

Finally, a thorough review of the literature enables you to become an expert in the area you are studying and a more knowledgeable teaching practitioner. This will guide you in all phases of your action research and enhance your ability to teach.

SOURCES FOR THE LITERATURE REVIEW

This section describes the kinds and number of sources that might be used in a review of the literature for an action research project.

Academic Journals

Academic journals are usually the best source for literature reviews. They contain articles written by specialists in the field (usually college professors) who describe their research, secondary research, novel applications of existing theories, or interesting new ideas set in a theoretical context. Hundreds of different academic journals are published in all areas, from medicine to psychology, cosmetology, farming, and education.

An academic journal is not the same as a magazine. Magazines are designed to attract a wide audience and generate profit. They are usually written by a staff of writers or reporters who often have little expertise in the subjects about which they are reporting. To report accurately about a subject of which you have little knowledge is difficult; thus, accuracy is often compromised. Also, magazines depend on advertising revenue, which does in some way affect what is published.

Academic journals, on the other hand, are designed to inform the field. Journal articles are written by scientists, researchers, and other academicians who send in their work to be considered for publication. Each article is then peer reviewed, which means it is critiqued by a jury of three to six experts in the field to check for accuracy and validity. Each reviewer makes a recommendation whether to accept the article for publication. Often many revisions are made before an article is finally accepted for publication. Also, most academic journals contain little or no advertising, and authors are required to cite and list all their sources.

The Internet

The Internet is a good place to find a great deal of information quickly; however, this information is not always credible. Whereas journal articles are peer reviewed before being published, the only criteria for putting information on the Internet is that one has a website and the technical knowledge to post it. Therefore, the Internet should always be used with caution because the information is not always credible.

The U.S. Department of Education maintains the ERIC website, at www. eric.ed.gov, which is designed specifically for educators. ERIC stands for Educational Resources Information Center. This site contains thousands of journal articles, research reports, curricula, conference papers, and teaching guides. Again, one must discriminate when selecting documents because the review process is minimal; thus, documents vary widely in their validity and credibility.

A physical disadvantage in using the Internet is that a computer monitor lets you see only a small bit of information at one time (usually only about 19 lines of text). This can be cumbersome and time consuming. Journal articles and books, however, allow you to take in a greater amount of text at one time, make notes in the margins, see the entire structure of a chapter or article, and quickly move back and forth through large sections of text.

Books

Books are fairly credible sources. Keep in mind, however, that just because information is printed in a book does not mean it is true. Books that cite their sources and those that are published by major publishing houses are generally those that can be trusted to provide credible information. Also, when using books, learn to skim and read only those chapters or parts that pertain to your research topic.

Nonprint Sources

Several nonprint sources can be used to provide background information for your action research project. You might want to find out what other teachers have done or experienced related to your topic and include their insights in your report. If you are looking at curriculum issues, curriculum coordinators usually are aware of the latest trends. Parents can provide insight related to the emotional issues of their children and tell you how their children are responding to or talking about school issues. Also, with a little searching you can often find community members or university-based researchers and teachers who have specialized knowledge related to your topic. For this last group, I have found that a short e-mail with a specific question is generally the most effective way to solicit insights.

How Many Sources?

Exactly how many sources or pieces of literature do you need for your literature review? Again, this is dictated solely by your research topic, the purpose of your research, and the type of research you are conducting. A master's thesis generally calls for 25 or more sources, and a doctoral dissertation, 50 or more sources. Smaller action research projects designed to be published in an academic journal, presented at a conference, shared with your peers, or conducted to fulfill a graduate course requirement might use from 2 to 15 sources. Moreover, many action research projects conducted for professional development or for evaluative or problem-solving purposes do not include a review of the literature and so do not use any sources.

SAMPLE LITERATURE REVIEWS

As stated in Chapter 3, the form that a literature review might take varies widely as to the form and the placement in your report. Below are two examples of literature reviews: one inserted at the beginning of an action research report and one at the end.

A Literature Review at the Beginning

I was interested in designing a new method to be used in identifying students for inclusion in gifted education programs in elementary schools. Below is a sample of part of the literature review that was included at the beginning of my action research report. This review gave me some ideas to use in designing my new identification method; it also lent credibility to my eventual design by putting it in a theoretical context. Nine sources are used here. The author and the year of publication of each of my sources are in parentheses. (Specific information related to citations, quotes, and the reference page can be found in *A Short Guide to Academic Writing* [Johnson, 2003a].)

IDENTIFYING STUDENTS FOR GIFTED EDUCATION PROGRAMS

The methods many schools use to identify students for gifted education services are not based on what is known about intelligence and creativity.

Intelligence

Howard Gardner (1996) defines intelligence as the ability to solve problems and create products that are valued within a cultural setting. Robert Sternberg (1996) describes it as knowing when and how to use analytic, creative, and practical abilities to reach a goal. Few in the fields of psychology or gifted education would define intelligence solely in terms of scores on standardized measures; yet IQ and achievement test scores are the predominant criteria for entrance into gifted education programs (Aamidor & Spicker, 1995; De Lieon, Argus-Calvo, & Medina, 1997; Hunsaker, Abeel, & Callahan, 1991; Richert, 1997). Identifying prospective students based solely on standardized quantitative measures does not reflect the latest theories related to intelligence, creativity, and productivity, yet schools continue to use such measures because their use is clean, efficient, and quantifiable. These methods are outdated and should not be used as the exclusive means for identification or acceptance into gifted education programs.

Creativity

Creativity is a cognitive process that leads to new or improved products, performances, or paradigms. It is a quality of thought that allows an individual to generate many ideas, invent new ideas, or recombine existing ideas in a novel fashion (Gallagher & Gallagher, 1994). Creativity is the ability to go beyond the given to generate novel and interesting ideas (Sternberg, 1996) or to produce something apart from the ordinary: something remarkable and something new (Feldman, Csikszentmihalyi, & Gardner, 1994). This is an important trait for achievement in all fields; however, the creative process is a trait that does not easily lend itself to measurement. Although standardized creativity tests may be able to identify students with creative capabilities such as the ability to generate many ideas or many different kinds of ideas, such measures cannot predict an individual's eventual creative achievement (Davis, 1997). The best predictor of future achievement, especially creative achievement, is past achievement (Davis, 1997; Sternberg, 1996). Therefore, it is reasonable to suggest that past performance be included within identification processes.

A Literature Review at the End

I could also wait until my data is collected, then compare my findings or recommendations to what others have written. The sample literature review below uses the same topic above—identification methods in a gifted education program; however, this literature review appears at the end of the action research report.

Recommendations

In reviewing my data, three recommendations are made for identifying students for our gifted education program.

1. *Make methods of identification consistent with your school's definition of giftedness.* A common definition of giftedness must precede any discussions related to methods of identification so that we are clear about what exactly we are trying to identify. Our district uses the U.S. Department of Education's (1993) definition in which a variety of talents are described including the visual and performing arts, creativity, specific academic areas, leadership, as well as intelligence. If we are not going to address all these areas with equal emphasis, we need to revise our definition.

2. *Use the threshold model to identify gifted students.* The threshold model describes a more inclusive method of defining and identifying gifted students (Davis, 1997; Piirto, 1994). Instead of using high criterion scores on intelligence tests for inclusion into gifted education programs (140 or above), students break a lower threshold (score of 115 to 120), as well as meet other types of criteria. This allows for a conception of giftedness that includes a variety of talents. The threshold model also complements Renzulli and Reis' (1997) schoolwide enrichment model. Anywhere from 10%–20% of the population are eligible to go to an enrichment center for special instruction.

3. *Use products and performances as one type of identifying criterion.* Identification for any type of special programming requires more than one type of measure or multiple criteria (Davis & Rimm, 1998; Richert, 1997). Students, teachers, or parents are allowed to make a case for inclusion by gathering a variety of evidence to support the need for special programming opportunities.

SUMMARY

- A review of the literature contains an examination and description of journal articles, Internet information, books, and other nonprint sources related to a particular topic.
- The literature review sets your topic in a theoretical context.
- A review of the literature enables you to connect education theory directly to your classroom practice.
- The number of sources used in a literature review is determined by your research topic and the type of research you are conducting.
- Some action research projects do not require a literature review.
- A review of the literature can be included at the beginning or the end of the action research report.

QUESTIONS AND ACTIVITIES

1. Find a topic you are interested in as a possible action research project. Find one journal article that contains a review of relevant literature at the beginning. What do you notice about the style of writing?
2. Using a topic that interests you, find and list one of each kind of the following sources: journal article, Internet website, book, and a nonprint source.
3. Find an example of an article in an academic journal that has a well-written literature review. Describe at least three things the author does well.
4. Use ERIC to find articles related to an area of interest.
5. Find an example of an article in a magazine and one related to a similar topic in an academic journal. What differences do you notice in the writing styles?

METHODS OF COLLECTING DATA

This chapter contains practical suggestions related to data collection techniques. Many of these techniques are also forms of authentic assessment that can also be used as part of your classroom teaching practice.

DATA COLLECTION

The goal of action research is to understand some element of your classroom by collecting data. Data (plural) are any form of information, observations, or facts that are collected or recorded. Collecting data is what separates the action research project from a newspaper editorial. As stated previously, action research is not simply writing about what you think to be true; rather, it is collecting data and making conclusions based on that data.

Systematic

In reviewing the literature related to action research, the one descriptor that is used in almost every book and article is the word *systematic*. Action research is systematic. This means that *before* the research begins a plan is in place that describes what data you will collect and when, how, and how often you will collect them. However, action research is a dynamic process; thus, it is common to abandon certain forms of data collection and adopt others as you are conducting the study.

One way to ensure that you are collecting data on a regular basis is to use a calendar or a checklist. Figure 8.1 shows a simple checklist that can be used to record which data were collected and when. This ensures that data are collected systematically and that all types of data are equally represented.

Data Collection and Soil Samples

Collecting data in an action research project is not a snapshot of a single incident like a test score. Nor should data collection rely on a single type of data, for example, collecting only survey data or only homework scores. Rather, action research is a

FIGURE 8.1   Checklist for Collecting Data

TYPE OF DATA	DATES COLLECTED						
Individual quiz scores	8/18	8/25	9/2	9/9	9/16		
Audiotapes	8/13	8/19	8/26	9/1	9/17		
Student writing samples	8/17	9/9	10/1				
Homework	8/11	8/17	8/23	8/27	9/2	9/10	9/16
Student journals	8/27	9/17					
Small-group conferences	8/20	8/27	9/3	9/10	9/17		

series of quick looks taken at different times and in a variety of ways. In this sense, data collection in action research is much like collecting soil samples: You collect little bits of soil in different places over time.

A Television Sports Analyst

In your action research project you are the lens through which a bit of classroom reality is described. It is a given that this reality will be filtered through your own experiences and perceptions; however, you have the responsibility to present an accurate portrayal and to be as unbiased as possible. Any biases of which you are aware should be stated up front so that readers of your report are able to take this into account. You are not creating a brochure for the Chamber of Commerce, nor are you advocating a particular methodology or approach; rather, you are examining what is happening in your classroom and letting us read your thoughts as you analyze what you are perceiving and experiencing. In this sense, you act as a television sports analyst for a football game as you describe what is happening and break it down so that others can understand it.

TYPES OF DATA COLLECTION IN ACTION RESEARCH

A wide variety of data to collect and methods used to collect them exist. This section describes 13 data collection methods. I would encourage you to select only two to four types of data to collect to keep your research focused. Nothing is more confusing than trying to read research that seems to go off in all sorts of directions.

Keep your action research simple and focused. Trying to collect too many kinds of data is also a good way to make your life miserable. Often, my graduate students find a lot of interesting ideas as they start their projects and want to go off chasing all of them. Those who do this usually end up making a mess of their research projects.

Finally, you may notice that some overlap or commonality exists between the methods described next. The goal is not to have categories and labels with precise edges; rather, it is to generate some ideas with fuzzy borders. In all cases in this chapter, and as I have continued to reiterate throughout this book, find or adapt the methods that best suit your research question or your teaching situation and that seem to make the most sense to you.

Log or Research Journal

A research journal is a notebook used to record thoughts and observations related to all parts of your research. Use this to describe each step of your research process. It is an important source of information to use when trying to piece together the chronology of your research project. You may choose to include a variety of data, such as observations, analyses, diagrams, sketches, quotes, student comments, scores, thoughts, or even feelings and impressions.

How you use your research journal and the form it takes is a matter of personal preference. Some choose to use their research journals to collect field notes and other forms of data whereas others keep their field notes separate and use the research journal to record their impressions and ideas related to the research process. I sometimes use a computer file as my research journal. The advantage of this is that it is quick and easy to organize and read, and I can print off copies or share disks with colleagues. The disadvantage is that I can usually see only 19 lines of print at any one time; I have to scroll up and down in linear fashion; I cannot draw or sketch; and it is less spontaneous. I suggest you choose the method that you will most likely continue using.

Field Notes—Your Observations

Field notes are the written observations of what you see taking place in your classroom. Beginning action researchers are often unsure of what they should record. My advice is to stop thinking and just write what you see. Once you start recording, you begin to see things that are interesting or important. In this way field notes help you notice details you might not otherwise have noticed. And as you make many observations over time, patterns begin to emerge from the data. Also, as stated in the previous chapter, a review of the literature may give you clues as to what kinds of things you might attend to in your field notes. Three types of field notes are described.

Thick Descriptions During.   The first type of field notes involves taking notes while teaching is taking place. However, very few teachers are able to check out during their teaching to become an objective observer recording thick descriptions of ongoing classroom events. Most need to be fully engaged in the teaching process and thus are not able to enter an effective researcher/recorder mode during teaching. Also, by becoming a researcher during your teaching you run the risk of becoming a nonteacher and, thus, becoming a foreign entity in your research environment. That is, by transforming yourself from a teacher, who regularly responds to students' immediate concerns, into an impartial researcher who observes and takes careful notes, you introduce something into the classroom environment that does not reflect what is normally there.

You can, however, observe another teacher's classroom or observe your own when somebody else is teaching. I have spent considerable time observing classrooms and taking field notes as both a researcher and a supervisor of preservice teachers in their field experiences. In this process I have learned much by watching master teachers at work. Providing training in some basic action research techniques and creating opportunities for teachers to do this each year is a very economical and effective form of teacher development. Here are five tips for observing a classroom and taking field notes:

1. *Enter the classroom as quickly and quietly as possible.* Move quickly to a spot in the classroom that offers the least distraction, and sit down. Usually this is in the back or to the side.

2. *If students ask you who you are, answer them.* "I'm Mr. Johnson from the college. I'm here to look at interesting things happening in your classroom." Students will attend to you for a short time, but you will quickly begin to fade from their consciousness.

3. *Begin taking notes without looking directly at students.* A person writing with his or her head down is much less distracting or imposing than a person staring and recording. Also, it is not always important that you see to know what is going on. It is possible to observe by listening and still get a good sense of a classroom setup, feelings, general impressions, and emotional tone. You can also record interesting or important dialogue by the teacher or students simply by listening.

4. *Smile.* A person smiling is much less threatening.

5. *Do not think—write.* Start by recording the time in the margin of your notes and then simply describe what you see happening. Whenever a new event or circumstance appears, record this time to provide a sense of chronology. Then write quickly without thinking. Working memory has a limited capacity, and it is difficult to perceive, record, process, and analyze information simultaneously. Writing quickly without thinking or analyzing frees up space in working memory and enables you to perceive more things.

Quick Notes During. Whereas it is difficult to record thick descriptions while you are teaching, it is possible to make quick notes to hold your ideas. Three tips for you to use are described:

1. *Keep a file in your desk drawer for every student with his or her name on it.* If something interesting occurs related to a particular student, make a quick note on the nearest scrap of paper, record the date, and put it in that student's file. Along with observations and field notes, these files can be used to collect representative samples of students' work, checklists, or test scores. The student file is a good data-collecting technique for action research, and at the same time it helps you become a more knowledgeable teacher when assessing growth, planning instruction, or speaking with parents about their child's progress.

2. *Keep a file related to the research project.* Whenever an idea, observation, or insight occurs to you during the day related to your research, make a quick note to yourself, record the date, and put it in your research file.

3. *Take notes on the margins or back of your lesson plans.* Often I am hit with a unique insight in the middle of a lesson. I find it most effective to make little notes to myself in the margin of my lesson plan. I use just enough words to hold the idea, then revisit it after class or after school when I am ready to record and write more fully. The more you do this, the better you will become at finding your original thoughts with single word clues.

Notes and Reflections After.   Like many teachers, I prefer to record my observations after the lesson or at the end of the day. I am more relaxed, I am not rushed for time, and I find that I am able to think and remember much more clearly. There are three ways you might do this:

1. *After each lesson, make a quick note to yourself in your research journal.* In my college classroom, I go back to my office after a class, shut the door, and scribble a few quick notes in my journal. When I have more time, I use these jottings to make more extensive field notes.

2. *Record your insights and observations at the end of the day.* It requires a certain amount of discipline to ensure that you do this on a regular basis. Set aside 10 minutes every day and make that time sacred.

3. *Reflect on the back of your lesson plans.* This becomes a good source of data telling you what was taught, when you taught it, how it was taught, how it went, and insights for change.

Checklists

Checklists come in many forms. A checklist is a list that specifies certain attributes, such as behaviors, traits, assignments, or skills. When that attribute is seen, some method is used to either check it off or indicate the number of times it was present.

Student Checklists.   Student checklists are checklists that are used by students. Ping Hew was using action research to study writing workshops in her fifth-grade class. As part of this, each student had a portfolio they were required to maintain that included, among other things, the weekly checklist in Figure 8.2. Each day of the workshop, students used tally marks to indicate the activities they participated in that day. The bottom three boxes are open ended, allowing for a variety of responses related to topics, skills, and questions. As the quarter progressed, these checklists gave Ping a very good sense of where her students were spending the

FIGURE 8.2   Student Checklist for Skills and Activities

Weekly Checklist for September 1–30, 1999

At the end of each class, put a tally mark behind any activities done in that session.

Generating/prewriting	
Drafting	
Revising	
Editing	
Conferencing/talking	
Reading	
Other	

Writing topics:

Special skills learned or used:

Things I have questions about:

majority of their time, of their writing topics, of the skills learned, and of the skills that needed to be taught.

Teacher Checklists.   Checklists can also be designed for use by teachers to indicate exactly what skills have been introduced or mastered and when. Checklists like these are also helpful in guiding instruction and providing evidence that skills have been covered. Figure 8.3 contains a teacher checklist for writing skills. One

FIGURE 8.3   Teacher Checklist for Writing

Writing Checklist for Second- and Third-Grade Students

Student: _____

Describe the student's progress using the following key: 3 = very much, 2 = some, 1 = very little, 0 = not at all.

ATTRIBUTES	DATES					
1. Uses invented spelling to hold ideas						
2. Can spell most words on the 100 MFW list						
3. Uses capital letters for beginning of sentences						
4. Uses periods and question marks						
5. Displays a willing attitude toward writing activities						
6. Is able to write attentively for about 15–20 minutes						
7. Is able to brainstorm ideas for writing						
8. Knows what nouns, verbs, and adjectives are						
9. Has ideas to share						
10. Is able to organize ideas						
11. Is able to talk about his or her writing						
12. Is able to write an acceptable rough (first) draft						
13. Is able to edit or revise the rough draft effectively						
14. Uses complete sentences						

Words per fifty (WPF) spelling scores:

Observations or comments:

checklist for each student is kept in a three-ring binder. The skills necessary for successful second- and third-grade writers are listed in the first column. During writing time or in individual writing conferences, it is a simple matter to take out this checklist and make a quick assessment.

An important note when using a teacher checklist: Do not try to cover all attributes during a single session; rather, look for a few attributes during each observation. Also, one observation tells you little; however, many short observations over time tell you much. Plan on using one checklist each quarter.

Open-Ended Checklists.   An open-ended checklist contains a list of skills with enough space for students to describe their ability, understanding, or usage of each skill (see Figure 8.4). This provides you with an accurate indicator of students' level of understanding and also enables you to plan instruction to meet specific needs.

Conferences and Interviews

There is an important difference between conferences and interviews. In a conference one or more students talk about their work or some aspect of classroom functioning. Prompts may be used to get students talking; however, lists of planned questions are not used. Conferences can be conducted individually or in small groups. In an interview students respond to planned questions, which are best conducted on an individual basis.

Individual Student Conferences.   Students should always do the majority of talking and lead the conversation in a conference. The exchange is open ended, and teacher questions are used simply as prompts to get students talking. Conferences can last anywhere from 2 to 15 minutes. Figure 8.5 contains a list of possible conference questions that can be used as prompts.

When conferencing with a student, take notes but do not try to get a verbatim transcript of the conference. Instead, record only those items you think are important, such as strengths, weaknesses, general impressions, skills learned, progress, insights, or what the student is currently working on. You may want to design some kind of a checklist to use for taking notes during conferences. Again, this is a matter of personal preference. It is normal to feel a little unsure of this process at first; however, after you have done it a few times you will get a good sense of what to record and how to best record it.

As a teaching tool, individual conferences are also an effective way to touch base with each student in a very personal way. For example, in Jason Hinkle's ninth-grade biology class, his students are assigned conference times to talk about their projects, which include a series of experiments and lab reports. Knowing they are going to meet with him, students are able to prepare and make sure they have something to say. In these short conferences, Jason listens, takes notes, asks questions, gives responses, encourages, and makes one or two suggestions for improving their experiments or lab reports. He schedules no more than three to five

FIGURE 8.4   Open-Ended Checklist

Writing Skills

SKILL	EXPLANATION OF HOW YOU USE EACH SKILL
Capitalization of names	
There versus their	
Adjectives	
Writing dialogue	
Paragraphs	
Commas	

FIGURE 8.5   Questions for Student Conferences

How's it going?
What are you working on?
Tell me about that.
What is something that you seem to do well?
What might be something that gives you problems? (Tell me about that.)
Read part of your story.
Do a long division problem, and talk out loud as you are doing it.
Tell me what you do when you work in a cooperative group.
What skills have you learned?
What part of science is most interesting to you?
What is something interesting or important that you have learned in our social studies class?

FIGURE 8.6   Checklist of Individual Conferences

Checklist for Individual Student Conference Dates

Billy A.	8/23	9/13	10/4			
Sally B.	8/23	9/13	10/4			
Amy C.	8/23	9/13	10/4			
Molly D.	8/24	9/14	10/11			
Michael E.	8/24	9/14	10/11			
Thomas F.	8/24	9/14	10/11			

conferences in any day because conferences can be wearing. This allows him to see each student every 2 weeks.

A checklist can be used to keep track of students and conference times (see Figure 8.6). Conferences such as these can be used across the curriculum as you work on teaching specific skills. They can also be used as a means of checking in and staying in touch with your students. Finally, conferences might also be used to address social issues or interpersonal issues within your classroom. You are limited only by your imagination.

Small-Group Conferences.   In a small-group conference you meet with three to eight students at one time. This is an effective data-collecting method in that you are able to see a number of students fairly quickly and watch them interacting with each other. It is also a valuable teaching tool because students are able to hear and respond to the thoughts of other students. Just like in the individual conference, the teacher should talk as little as possible.

Small-group conferences can also be adapted for use in a variety of situations. For example, it may be used to discuss subjects such as good books, current or historical events, research projects, writing projects, moral dilemmas, math skills, problem-solving skills, textbook reading assignments, homework problems, or personal issues. You cannot, however, assume that students instinctively know how to function in small groups. Thus, structure must be provided so that they know how to speak and respond to each other (see Figure 8.7). It is common to spend a few class sessions teaching students how to interact in small groups and to use students to help model the process. Each group can use a checklist to report their progress (Appendix G). This helps the group focus on the key elements of successful group behavior and provides you with another form of data (see Figure 8.8).

Interviews.   An interview differs from a conference in that an interview has a specific set of questions prepared in advance and is teacher directed. The questions should be asked in the same order each time to maintain consistency.

FIGURE 8.7   Rules for Small-Group Conferences

Before

1. Be prepared.
2. Bring all materials with you.

Speaking

1. Only one person talks at a time.
2. Say what you have to say, then let others respond.
3. Do not dominate the conversation.
4. Listen.

Responding

1. Ask a question.
2. Find something you like.
3. Ask for clarification.
4. Find something it reminds you of.
5. Offer suggestions or ways to do it differently.
6. Do not make put-downs or personal remarks.

Figure 8.9 demonstrates a hierarchy of questions, going from lower-order closed-response questions to higher-order open-ended questions. Make sure to include both types in your interview.

A common mistake most beginning interviewers make is having too many questions. Keep your interviews short (you can always ask follow-up questions). End each interview with an open-ended question, such as, Is there anything else that you want to say about . . . ? Finally, do not try to take detailed field notes

FIGURE 8.8   Checklist for Small-Group Conferences

Group: _____   Date: _____

	yes	no	some
1. The group stayed on task.			
2. Everyone responded or asked a question.			
3. The group used time wisely.			
4. Everyone was prepared for the conference.			

INTERESTING OR IMPORTANT IDEAS
1.
2.
3.

FIGURE 8.9   Hierarchy of Interview Questions

1. Which would you rather read? (a) fiction, (b) science fiction, (c) nonfiction, (d) historical fiction, or (e) mysteries 2. What is your favorite reading genre? 3. Name a very good book or your favorite book. 4. Tell me what you like to read. 5. Tell me about your reading.	closed-response 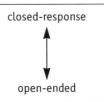 open-ended

during the interview; rather, write down only a few interesting ideas or impressions. Keep your focus on the responses and follow-up questions. Use an audiotape to record the interview (videotape is too obtrusive), then go back and take detailed notes.

Video- and Audiotapes

Videotapes provide you with information related to students' nonverbal behaviors, their location or movement throughout a lesson, and a general overview of your performance or pedagogical techniques. However, as stated in an earlier chapter, a video camera is an obtrusive instrument, and thus it creates a nonreal teaching environment. One way to diminish this effect is by videotaping a great deal so that students get used to the camera. Another way is to use audiotapes. Audiotapes are quicker, easier, less intrusive, more natural, and easy to listen to in a car or with a small handheld unit. Although you might miss nonverbal behaviors and movement, you will find that you get just as much important information with an audiotape.

Data Retrieval Charts

Data retrieval charts (DRC) are visual organizers that are used to help you (or your students) collect and organize information. These can come in a variety of forms. As part of an inquiry project, the students in Pam Bauer's fifth-grade class created the DRC in Figure 8.10 to determine the kinds of desserts chosen by students. Tally

FIGURE 8.10   DRC for Analyzing Dessert Choices

Use tally marks to indicate the number of times each dessert was chosen.

Pie	
Cake	
Cookie	
None	

FIGURE 8.11   DRC for Dessert Choices Sorted by Gender

	FEMALES	MALES
Pie		
Cake		
Cookie		
None		

marks were used to indicate the number of times each dessert was chosen. This DRC provided data that could then be quantified and compared across grade level or over time. Gender differences can easily be compared by including an extra column (Figure 8.11).

Rating Checklist

A rating checklist specifies traits you are looking for in a product or performance and allows the observer to assign levels of performance to each trait. This is similar to a rubric; however, whereas a rubric uses a sentence or more to provide a description of each level, a rating checklist uses one-word indicators (see Figure 8.12). I find rating checklists to be a more pragmatic method to use for collecting data for action research and for use in classroom assessment. The rating checklist in Figure 8.12 was used at the end of a science unit. Students evaluated their own level of performance on one side, and the teacher evaluated their performance on the other.

Students' Products or Performances

Samples of students' work can be used as data sources. Remember that you do not need to collect every bit of students' work; rather, only take representative samples at different time periods to give you a feel for students' performances and their change over time. It is often helpful to create a flexible schedule to determine when you will collect students' work before you begin.

Product and Performance.   Figure 8.13 shows a product and performance assessment form (PPAF). This rating checklist can be used to analyze and evaluate any type of product or performance, such as science projects, inventions, dramas, dances, or experiments (Appendix H). Incidentally, all forms described in this chapter can be used by both students and teachers. Just like teachers (Watts & Johnson, 1995), students who analyze and assess their own work become more critical and skillful practitioners.

FIGURE 8.12 **Rating Checklist for Science Skills**

Science Skills

Key: 4 = outstanding; 3 = very good; 2 = average; 1 = low

STUDENT	SKILL	TEACHER
	Observe and describe	
	Create a graph	
	Weighing	
	Predicting	
	Organize data—create groups	
	Conclude	
	Use a lab report	

Student: _____

Teacher: _____

Grade: _____

Comments:

Writing Samples. Figure 8.14 contains a rating checklist that can be used to analyze and evaluate any type of writing (Appendix I). This is also a good teaching tool in that it forces you to define exactly what is expected and it puts the onus on you to teach each skill associated with those expectations. Also, students appreciate knowing what the requirements are and getting the precise feedback that this form provides.

Independent Research Projects. Figure 8.15 shows a rating checklist used for students' independent research projects (Appendix J). Notice that all the elements of action research are found on this checklist. Understanding action research will enable you to incorporate more effectively methods of science, inquiry, and research into your own teaching, and also provide you with a variety of ideas to use in getting students to create their own independent research projects.

FIGURE 8.13   Product and Performance Assessment Form

Product and Performance Assessment Form

Student: _____   Age: _____

Grade: _____   Type of Product or Performance: _____

Key: 5 = very high; 4 = high; 3 = average; 2 = low; 1 = very low

When compared to other students of a similar age, rate the product or performance on the following criteria:

1. Creativity _____

2. Integration of ideas ____

3. Technical merit ____

4. Sophistication and level of detail ____

5. Aesthetics: artistic expression, emotion, feeling ____

6. Overall effect ____

Comments:

FIGURE 8.14   Writing Assessment Form

Writing Assessment Form

Writing prompt:

Key: 5 = very high; 4 = high; 3 = average; 2 = low; 1 = very low

content, ideas _____	mechanics: spelling, grammar, punctuation _____	met deadlines; fulfilled assignment requirements _____
organization, structure _____	fluency, communication _____	appearance _____

Ideas or insights:

Skills to work on:

FIGURE 8.15   Checklist for Independent Research

Checklist for Independent Research Projects

Key: 3 = trait is present to a high degree; 2 = trait is present;
1 = trait is present to a low degree; 0 = trait is not present

___ A question was asked, a problem was identified, or an area of exploration was defined.

___ Data collection was systematic.

___ Data was analyzed in a way that made it credible and trustworthy.

___ The results were described clearly and accurately.

___ Recommendations or conclusions were made based on the results.

___ The research project was linked to a theoretical context.

___ The research was communicated in a way that was understandable.

___ Met all deadlines and requirements.

Focus of the action research:

Major results and conclusions:

Scores and Other Quantifiable Data.   Students' scores on tests, homework, quizzes, grades, and standardized assessment measures can also be used as a data source. However, they should never be used as the only source of data.

Surveys

Surveys allow you to get a variety of information quickly. They can be designed using both closed-response or open-ended questions.

Closed-Response Questions.   A closed-response question provides a number of choices for respondents to select. An example follows:

```
What is your favorite reading genre? (a) history,
(b) comedy, (c) science fiction, (d) mystery
```

The advantage of this type of question is that you can ask a number of questions and get quantifiable data on many types of issues. For example, after surveying a group of students with the question above, one could safely report that 84.4% of students surveyed preferred comedy as a reading genre. The problem with these kinds of questions is that they can be inaccurate, misleading, or controlling. What if the first reading choice of a respondent was not even listed in the question above? Or what if a respondent liked to read three or four different kinds of books equally well?

Open-Ended Questions.   An open-ended question allows respondents unlimited choices. An example follows:

```
What kinds of books do you like to read?
```

These questions provide a more accurate sense of what respondents are actually thinking. Some respondents may report four or five different kinds of books whereas others may report only one. The researcher would then create categories out of all the books listed and report the number of books in each category (see inductive analysis in Chapter 9). This data might be reported as in the following:

```
Forty-five students provided 152 responses to the
survey question. The greatest number of responses
(49%) indicated realistic fiction as the preferred
genre.
```

Problems with open-ended survey questions are that they are somewhat messy in terms of analysis and you can generally ask fewer of them.

Tips for Preparing Surveys.   The following tips will help you in preparing surveys:

1. *Do not use too many questions or questions that are not necessary.* I have found that using four to eight questions is most effective. Too many questions frustrate respondents. A frustrated respondent will not complete the survey or will not give you accurate information. Err on the side of using too few rather than too many questions.
2. *Make your questions short, concise, and reader friendly.* If a reader has to work to figure out exactly what you are asking, chances are that the question will not be read, or, if it is, it will be misunderstood.
3. *Proofread your questions several times.* Make sure the questions say exactly what you intend.
4. *Be very clear with your questions.* Always assume the reader knows nothing.
5. *Do not use leading questions.* A good survey is completely objective. Respondents should not know your position on any of the issues asked about.
6. *Always include at least one open-ended question.* If you are using closed-response questions, provide an opportunity for respondents to make comments at the end.
7. *Create a neat, professional-looking document.* The presentation should be attractive, well organized, and easy to read.

Attitude and Rating Scales

Attitude and rating scales provide respondents with a question or statement for which they are asked to select one of several answers that determines the strength of their response.

Attitude Scales.   Students' attitudes are assessed by asking them to respond to a series of statements in a way that indicates their level of agreement or disagreement. Attitude scales like this can quickly provide you with information about students' attitudes and yield quantitative data that can be used to make comparisons. A 5-point rating scale is usually most effective for students in grades 3 and above.

```
Key: SA = strongly agree; A = agree; NO = no opinion;
         D = disagree; SD = strongly disagree

1. Reading is fun: SA . . . A . . . NO . . . D . . . SD
```

These responses can also be numbered to provide you with quantitative data.

```
Key: 5 = strongly agree; 4 = agree; 3 = no opinion;
         2 = disagree; 1 = strongly disagree

1. Reading is fun:                 5 .. 4 .. 3 .. 2 .. 1
2. I know how to use science skills: 5 .. 4 .. 3 .. 2 .. 1
```

With younger students, provide fewer choices and use graphics.

```
1. I like to read: very much ☺, some ☺, little ☹.
```

Rating Scales.   A rating scale is used to determine the strength of a response. These are often used to determine how much, how often, or how many times something occurs.

```
Key: 4 = often; 3 = some; 2 = little; 1 = not at all

1. I read at home each day:          4 .. 3 .. 2 .. 1
2. I watch TV at home each day:      4 .. 3 .. 2 .. 1
3. I complete my homework at school: 4 .. 3 .. 2 .. 1
4. I use some sort of prewriting
   strategy:                         4 .. 3 .. 2 .. 1
```

The Arts

The arts are another way of seeing the world and can be used to bring a different level of understanding to your action research. Elliot Eisner (1998) suggests that literature and poetry be used as a research device to capture and illuminate some portion of reality. Artists and researchers are very much alike in that the work of both are like lenses through which reality is interpreted and translated.

Certain kinds of art lend themselves naturally to action research. These include (a) two-dimensional visual art, such as sketches, collage, paintings, drawings, and photography and (b) the language arts, such as poetry, creative writing, short story, drama, and written dialogue. You might also include students' use of these mediums along with your analysis. I would encourage you to experiment with the arts as one of your data sources. Your credibility will not be diminished if you collect multiple forms of data and if you include an analysis of your artistic data.

Archival Data

Archival data include past grades, test scores, cumulative folders, health records, parental occupation, or attendance records. Make sure you follow your school procedures for obtaining access to this data, and that they are used and reported in an ethical manner.

Websites, Class Journals, or E-Mail

Websites.   Websites can be used to create a living, dynamic classroom entity. Students can log on to a specific site and read and respond to what others have said on a given topic. The transaction can be printed for use as a data source.

Class Journals.   The class journal is a nontechnical version of the website. Simply provide a blank notebook that is passed around the class or put in a learning center for several weeks. Students then enter their thoughts, ideas, impressions, or any other forms of response such as pictures or diagrams. You may need to provide some guidelines and check in quite often so that this does not turn into a form of graffiti that might be highly offensive to some. The website and class journal are very effective methods to use in getting to the underbelly of classroom discourse.

E-Mail.   E-mail is a quick, easy, and private form of communication between a student and teacher. In my courses, I usually assign students a certain number of e-mail messages to write to me during the semester. These messages allow me access to students' thinking and provide valuable insight in the planning of my classes. In action research, students could e-mail you on a variety of topics.

SUMMARY

- Data are any form of information, observations, or facts that are collected or recorded.
- A flexible plan for collecting data should be in place before you begin collecting them.
- The data collected in action research should be varied and collected in different ways over time.
- There are a wide variety of data that could be collected; however, selecting only two to four kinds will keep your action research focused.

QUESTIONS AND ACTIVITIES

1. Go to an interesting place. Practice taking field notes by recording what you see. Plan on spending at least 30 minutes at this place on two or more occasions.
2. Pick an assignment or project that you have your students do or that you plan to do with them. Create a checklist that has the specific skills or attributes necessary to complete the assignment.
3. Create a short open-ended checklist for students and experiment by using it with one class or subject area.
4. Think of an area or topic you are interested in. Create an interview with four to eight questions. Interview one or more students or adults using follow-up questions you feel are appropriate. Tape-record your interview.
5. Use an audiotape to record one of your classes. What did you discover? Based on this tape, create a DRC to indicate the number and type of some observation. For example, the level of question, the gender of those who were asked or who responded to the questions, the number of times you said the word *um*, or the number of positive statements.
6. What are five characteristics or qualities of a good movie? Use these to create a ratings checklist. Evaluate two to four recent movies. You may want to do this in small groups. This can be extended to TV shows, dramas, or any other performance.
7. Create a rating checklist for a student product or performance that you plan to have your students do.
8. Create a survey related to any topic that interests you. Experiment with different types of questions and have at least five people respond to it. If you are reading this book as part of a class, you may want to bring your survey to class and practice by responding to each other's surveys.
9. Go to an interesting place. Describe that place using visual art or a form of language art.

METHODS OF
ANALYZING DATA

This chapter describes data analysis. Analysis means to break something down into its component parts so that it can be understood. In action research, data are analyzed and organized into categories so that others might come to understand the reality you are trying to represent. Three elements related to data analysis are presented in this chapter: (a) accuracy and credibility; (b) validity, reliability, and triangulation; and (c) inductive analysis.

ACCURACY AND CREDIBILITY: THIS IS WHAT IS

The ultimate goal of action research is to use your findings to make effective changes or choices. To this end, the collection and analysis of data must be accurate and credible. Accuracy in action research means that the data you are collecting creates a fairly true picture of the bit of reality you are observing. This helps you make decisions that are best for your particular situation. Credibility in action research means trustworthy or capable of being believed. This enables you and others to use your data with confidence. The following seven tips will help you establish more accuracy and credibility as you collect and analyze your data:

1. *Record your observations carefully and precisely.* Always double-check to make sure you are recording exactly what you are seeing.

2. *Describe all phases of data collection and analysis.* In your recording, recount all the steps used in collecting and analyzing the data. In your eventual reporting you want to create a level of clarity whereby another person could duplicate your steps.

3. *Make sure you record and report everything that is of importance.* Record and report fully; do not omit data that may be counter to what you believe. The goal is to understand fully all aspects of what you are observing.

4. *Be as objective as possible in describing and interpreting what you see.* Pronounced biases or hidden agendas are fairly easy to spot and prevent you from seeing all aspects of what you are trying to study. They also make your action research less accurate and credible.

5. *Use enough data sources.* (See Triangulation below.) Your observations and analysis will be much more accurate and credible if you are able to find similar patterns using two or more forms of data. For a short observation (2 to 4 weeks), I usually ask my students to use a minimum of two sources. For longer action research projects, the number of sources is dictated by the question and the kinds of data you are trying to collect.

6. *Use the right kinds of data sources.* (See Validity below.) The type of data you choose to collect should provide the most accurate understanding possible of your research topic. For example, if I were interested in understanding how middle school students use humor, I might interview classroom teachers. Although this could provide some interesting information, the data would be a poor reflection of the reality I was trying to observe. A much more accurate and credible view would be obtained by using audiotapes of actual conversations, by observing middle school students and taking descriptive field notes, and by creating a survey form in which students self-report to indicate the kinds of humor used and the instances in which it was used.

7. *Look long enough and deep enough.* A 3-week observation might provide some interesting data; however, a 3-month observation would make your data even more accurate and credible. Longer observations provide more chances to see and confirm patterns than do shorter observations. Again, the length of your observation and data collection is dictated solely by your question. The final criterion should always be the degree to which you have created an accurate picture of what was studied.

VALIDITY, RELIABILITY, AND TRIANGULATION

Three essential parts of establishing accuracy and credibility in any research project are validity, reliability, and triangulation. In action research, they take on a different form than they do in traditional experimental research.

Validity

How do we know your data actually assess and describe what they say they do? Validity is the degree to which a thing measures what it reports to measure. For example, in trying to assess the writing ability of elementary students, I could give them a standardized test of grammar and punctuation in which they would read a series of questions and choose one of four responses. This would produce some fairly accurate results that could be quantified and used to make comparisons; however, this type of measure does not look at writing in an authentic context, and thus, it is not a very valid measure of students' ability to organize and communicate their ideas using writing. A more valid assessment would be to look at students' actual writing samples and use the writing assessment form described in Chapter 8 to rate specific elements.

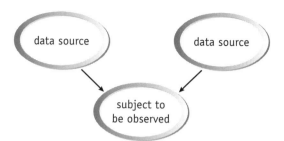

FIGURE 9.1   Triangulation

Triangulation

Triangulation means looking at something from more than one perspective. Think of a triangle with the subject to be observed as one point and the various data sources as the other two points (see Figure 9.1). Triangulation ensures that you are seeing all sides of a situation. It also provides greater depth and dimension, thereby enhancing your accuracy and credibility. In action research, triangulation is achieved by collecting different types of data, using different data sources, collecting data at different times, and by having other people review your data to check for accuracy and adjust your findings.

Reliability

Reliability is the degree to which a study or experiment can be repeated with similar results. Unlike action research, traditional experimental research strives to create a hermetically sealed world with all the variables controlled so that X can be said to cause Y beyond all doubt. If the experiment is reliable, X should cause Y each time it is repeated. If this is indeed the case, the experiment is deemed reliable, the results are generalized to similar situations, and the researcher is granted tenure at a major university.

Action researchers, however, observe messy, real-world events in which humans are mucking about. These humans are inherently and wondrously unpredictable and not at all inclined to exist in hermetically sealed worlds. Thus, each time we search and research we expect to see different things. The closest we come to repetition is noticing recurring items, themes, or patterns that emerge from our data. (See Inductive Analysis below.) Therefore, action research findings are not generalized broadly; instead they are used to help understand particular situations as well as inform similar situations.

INDUCTIVE ANALYSIS

Inductive analysis means to look at a field or group of data and try to induce or create order by organizing what is observed into groups. This should occur as you begin to collect data. Look for recurring items, themes, or patterns to emerge. Similar things should be coded and moved into initial categories. These categories, however, should be very flexible as later data may change their nature and composition. It is helpful to begin this process while you are collecting data because the categories that form initially inform further data collection.

Larry, Moe, and Curly Help with Inductive Analysis

Let me use the Three Stooges to illustrate inductive analysis. I watched a Three Stooges video to understand the Stooges and their humor. My initial questions were, What kind of humor is found? Of what are these episodes comprised? Who are the Stooges? (Note how these questions help inform and provide focus for my search.)

I watched a short 15-minute episode on videotape called *Grips, Grunts, and Groans* (Columbia Pictures, 1937) and began to look for instances of humor. (The events in a Three Stooges episode happen much faster than in real life; thus, I used the pause button often to suspend video reality to make notes.) As I watched, I used field notes to record those funny things I saw. *Funny things* (humor), in this instance, was defined as those elements inserted into the movie for the express purpose of creating a comedic effect. As I watched, my notes began to look like the following:

> Bump, stumble, kick, punch, slap, poke, twist ear, word play silly, absurd silly, word play silly, absurd silly, etc.

After the first time through the video, I saw that the types of humor recorded in my notes could be put into four categories.

Thing-to-Head Violence.   This violence represents instances where a nonhuman thing hit or was dropped on somebody's head. For example, Larry hits Moe on the head with a board or an anvil falls on Curly's head.

Human-to-Human Violence.   A part of somebody's body was struck, twisted, or otherwise violently engaged by a part of somebody else's physical being. This violence included instances of eye poking, ear twisting, kicks, chokes, punches, pushes, slaps, or general violence such as twisting one's foot.

Self-Mishap.   These are instances in which characters cause their own mishap, including stumbles, bumps, or falling episodes.

Silly Stuff.   Silly stuff represents those items, events, phrases, or actions that are incongruous, apart from what is normally expected, or reflect an exaggeration of what normally is. An example of situational silliness would be the Stooges accidentally pulling off the pants of a drunk wrestler while trying to drag him, revealing funny, long underwear with garters. An example of verbal silliness would be what is said after a man throws water on the Stooges who were just knocked unconscious by blows to the head. Curly yells out, "Man the lifeboats." Moe says, "Woman and children first." The implication is that the Stooges acted as if they were on a boat that was sinking.

Each category contained different types of humor. Once I had my initial categories and subcategories, I created a version of an open-ended checklist (see Figure 9.2). I then viewed the episode a second time and put a tally mark next to each type of humor every time I observed it.

I was thus able to break down the humor into its component parts and get a good sense of what the total episode comprised. It looks as if, more than anything, the Three Stooges material was violent. Forty-three instances of humor were violence inflicted on another person (human-to-human and thing-to-head violence); however, silliness was the largest single category of humor. In this episode, the Stooges were sillier than I had imagined they would be; however, the amount of violence stands out to the viewer watching in the twenty-first century. To add credibility to my observation and analysis I viewed this particular video several times. I also had somebody else view it to see whether they came up with similar categories and numbers.

This inductive analysis gave me a good understanding of this single episode of the Stooges and their humor. To extend this study, I would need to observe several Stooges episodes and use the same categories to collect and organize data. This data would then be put in the form of a bar graph for easy consumption by the reader. This would also allow me to compare various Stooges episodes or to compare the Stooges to other comedians of that era or today. I might also choose to

FIGURE 9.2   Three Stooges Humor

SILLY STUFF		HUMAN-TO-HUMAN VIOLENCE		THING-TO-HEAD VIOLENCE		SELF-MISHAP	
Situational silliness:	26	General hurt:	5	Things dropped on head:	12	Bump or stumble:	9
Verbal silliness:	7	Slap:	5	Things hit on head:	11		
		Kick:	4				
		Twist ear:	2				
		Poke eye:	2				
		Punch:	2				
		Choke:	1				
		Push:	1				
Total:	33	Total:	22	Total:	23	Total:	9

investigate further to see whether early Stooges and late Stooges differ. I might want to pursue other questions: Did the type of humor change over time? Did the Stooges get more violent over time? Did they get more silly over time? Do HPM (humor-per-minute) ratios of the Stooges differ in various eras? Do males react differently than females to Stooges humor? (You may notice that a good study usually creates as many questions as answers.)

Case Studies or Representative Samples

In my report I will use representative samples to bring further understanding to the Stooges reality that I observed. I will include a few examples of the funny things in each category so that the reader fully understands what that category entails. Including representative samples also allows the reader to go beyond the numbers, to make the research come alive.

Verbal Silliness

The scene opens with two railway security guards walking, clubs in hand, by a train car marked *horses*. One foreman taps on the door and says, "Anybody in there?" Curly's high, whining voice is heard, "Nobody here but us horses." The two guards, having gotten an answer to their question, begin walking away. After two steps, they realize the incongruity, stop, do a double take, and wait for the door to open.

Verbal Silliness

A gangster has made a big bet on Gustov, a professional wrestler. The Stooges have been paid by the gangster to keep him from getting drunk for that evening's match. Gustov is about to drink a large container of something when Moe says, "Listen, Gustov, you can't drink that. That's alcohol." Gustov snorts and says, "That's not alcohol. That's just a little tequila, vodka, and cognac." Curly says, "Oh, that's different. Go ahead." Gustov pours the jug down his throat. The bit of incongruity is that although tequila, vodka, and cognac are not referred to as alcohol, they all contain it.

Situational Silliness

Curly goes mad every time he smells Wild Hyacinth. In a restaurant, a woman accidentally pours some on him. Curly begins making high-pitched "woo, woo, woo" sounds. He slaps his forehead repeatedly, barks, and makes wild twisting, dancing motions with his legs. He goes crazy, trips over a table, and starts breaking a chair, then yells, "Moe, Larry, tickle my foot!" Larry and Moe tackle him, twist his legs, yank off his shoes, and begin tickling his feet. There is much flopping around and manic laughing by Curly and he eventually comes to his senses.

Self-Mishap

Running from the two railway guards, the Stooges round a corner. Two women are standing next to a baby carriage. In unison, the Stooges trip over the baby carriage and fall face first on the sidewalk.

Human-to-Human Violence

Moe tells Curly to put up his hands. He then hits him in the stomach. When Curly makes a sound in protest, Moe uses his fist to pound him on top of the head, twists and slaps his nose, and slaps his forehead. Curly yells in a loud, high voice, "Ow, ow, ow . . . ohhhh!"

Thing-to-Head Violence

In the locker room before the big wrestling match, Larry, Moe, and Curly have finally succeeded in getting Gustov, the drunk professional wrestler, ready to go out and wrestle. They then accidentally knock him into a set of lockers. Five dumbbells that are on top of the lockers fall, one at a time, on Gustov's head.

Vision Quest

As another example of inductive analysis, I was interested in examining the idealized visions of the undergraduate students in my literacy methods course. That is, how did they see themselves teaching literacy when they got their own classroom teaching position? During student teaching I have often noticed a certain amount of stress when the idealized teaching visions of student teachers do not match their current teaching reality. For this action research project I was interested in seeing what the initial idealized vision was and how it changed throughout the semester as a result of my instruction and their field experiences.

Twenty-five students were in my undergraduate literacy methods course, 22 females and 3 males. Most of the students were in their early twenties; however, two females and one male were in their late thirties or early forties. To get at their idealized visions, I gave them the following writing prompt: "Imagine yourselves 5 years from now. You are in a regular classroom teaching some aspect of literacy. What do you see? What's going on? What does it look like?"

Students wrote one to two paragraphs on a sheet of paper. I collected them and analyzed this data, looking for patterns. This was repeated at 1-month intervals four times during the semester. I called this Vision Quest. The following are some examples of students' responses:

8/31/99

I see myself stressing meaning and feeling within the message and words of books. I will probably assign or suggest books with these characteristics—books that share good family ties, struggle, success, hard work, etc.   [female]

In 5 years I see my students participating in short skits or role plays to share what a book was about or an individual chapter. The plays will be written and directed by the students themselves (with help as needed). [female]

In 5 years I see myself modeling quiet reading time for my students. I also see myself incorporating reading into other subject areas. I do not see myself doing comprehension sheets or book reports.   [female]

I see myself teaching second grade. The students are seated on the floor next to me while I introduce our book. They listen to me read while they follow along in their book. Then they have the opportunity to explain the story in their own words, with a story board, or acting it out. Later, they will be able to write about the story, perhaps including themselves. They will be able to draw pictures. These will be displayed.   [female]

As I read through students' descriptions, I looked for patterns, themes, or similar kinds of things. For instance, many students described aspects of creating a warm, inviting classroom environment. In my notes I jotted down *warm-fuzzy, environment, atmosphere* as an initial category. Every time I found something related to creating a warm, comfortable environment, I put a tally mark by this descriptor. I read all the selections and made adjustments to my initial categories. Figure 9.3 shows which categories and subcategories I used. I then went through the data a second time and once again put a tally mark every time an instance of an activity fell within that category. This twice-through approach allowed for more accuracy.

Defining and Describing Categories

One cannot expect the reader to have complete understanding of my categories, so, just as with the Three Stooges, I must define and describe each category. To demonstrate I have included the following examples:

Holistic or Nontraditional

This category represents activities that might fit within a whole-language classroom, specifically, activities that would *not* reflect a basal or skills-based approach. The subcategories include:

Reading choices.   Students would be able to make choices about the kinds of books they want to read.

Creative projects.   Activities would include drama, role play, art, games, and puppets.

FIGURE 9.3   Vision Quest, First Month

I. Warm Environment	**6**
II. Holistic/Nontraditional Activities	**16**
A. Reading choices	4
B. Creative projects	3
C. Student-centered activities	4
D. Class library/books	2
E. Independent reading	3
III. Skills-Oriented/Traditional Activities	**23**
A. Vocabulary instruction	4
B. Basals and worksheets	8
C. Teacher-led discussion	3
D. Round-robin reading	8
IV. Teacher Reading to Class	**8**
V. Specific Pedagogical Methods	**2**

Student-centered activities.   Students would be in charge of a process or a final product or performance. For example, students would write and direct their own plays, or students would be able to retell a story in their own words using a storyboard.

Class library/books.   A prescribed place in the classroom with lots of books would be set aside as a reading area.

Independent reading.   Time would be scheduled for students to read books of their choice independently.

Below is an example of how I might put the data into categories:

I see myself sitting in a cozy chair with my students sitting on a large soft rug in front of me. [*Warm Environment*] In my hands I hold a brand-new book. I introduce the book to the children and I begin to read aloud. [*Teacher Reading to Class*] When I have finished reading, we discuss the book. [*Teacher-Led Discussion*]   [female]

I see myself in 5 years with a large selection of books that I have read and am comfortable with. [*Class Library/Books*] Students choose their own books. [*Reading Choices*] I will allow ample class reading time. [*Independent Reading*]   [female]

I see myself helping students learn new words by using overheads. As a class we would read the words together, then use them in sentences. [*Vocabulary Instruction*] I just think it will be exciting to have them learn new words.   [female]

I see myself reading to students every day. [*Teacher Reading to Class*] Students in my classroom will have free time to read every day. [*Independent Reading*] Perhaps there will be a special reading corner. [*Warm Environment*] I plan to use trade books in reading class and across the curriculum. I really like that idea. I would like to have a large library in my classroom. [*Class Library/Books*]   [female]

I see myself setting up a small library in my classroom where children are able to read when they are done with their work. [*Class Library/Books*] I would make my library full of color, pictures of books, and many comfortable chairs to create an inviting reading environment that would make children look forward to reading. [*Warm Environment*]   [female]

The Next Month

The next month the same categories were used. As you might expect, the change reflects my instruction, the literacy philosophy I was proposing, and students' interaction with these ideas (see Figure 9.4). In Chapter 18 you can see how this

FIGURE 9.4   Vision Quest, Second Month

I. Warm Environment		**11**
II. Holistic/Nontraditional Activities		**64**
A. Reading choices	24	
B. Creative projects	12	
C. Student-centered activities	5	
D. Class library/books	5	
E. Independent reading	18	
III. Skills-Oriented/Traditional Activities		**9**
A. Vocabulary instruction	1	
B. Basals and worksheets	3	
C. Teacher-led discussion	5	
D. Round-robin reading	0	
IV. Teacher Reading to Class		**15**
V. Specific Pedagogical Methods		**17**

data was reported in graph form. One final thought: Methods used for inductive analysis vary and are a matter of personal preference. And although it might seem very messy at first, you will get more comfortable with this process by doing it.

SUMMARY

- Analysis means to break down something into its component parts so that it can be understood.
- The collection and analysis of data must be accurate and credible to be of use in making effective changes or choices.
- Validity is the degree to which a thing measures what it reports to measure.
- Triangulation means collecting more than one form of data or looking at something from more than one perspective.
- Reliability is the degree to which a study or experiment can be repeated with similar results.
- Action researchers recognize that the universe they are observing is a messy, unreliable entity, and thus, they look for repeating patterns and themes to help them understand it.
- Inductive analysis means to observe a field and create order by organizing items into groups or categories.
- In using inductive analysis, initial categories should be flexible as later data may change their nature and composition.

QUESTIONS AND ACTIVITIES

1. Cut out a newspaper article, a description of research, or a research article that you feel lacks credibility. Tell why.
2. Find an interesting person or student to observe for a short time. Use two of the data sources described in Chapter 8 to create understanding.
3. Cut out an ad in a newspaper or magazine that you feel lacks validity. Tell why.
4. Practice inductive analysis by randomly generating a list of 25 nouns. Then, in a small group or individually, put order to this field by moving them into groups or categories. Describe your field in terms of categories and numbers in each category.
5. Go to a place that is interesting and unique where you can observe people. Use field notes to record the behaviors you see. Then use inductive analysis to put order to your data. Report your data in terms of categories and numbers in each category.
6. Extend the previous activity by creating a checklist or data retrieval chart that uses the categories described. Go back to your interesting place at a different time of day. Use tally marks to record the instances of behaviors you observe.

Add new categories if you need to. Create a graph to compare and report your observations and conclusions.

7. To extend the previous activity further, use the same checklist or data retrieval chart to observe a different but similar place. Create a bar graph to compare and report your observations and conclusions.

QUANTITATIVE DESIGN IN ACTION RESEARCH

Quantitative research is based on the collection and analysis of numerical data. Earlier it was said that action research falls clearly in the realm of qualitative research because it does not manipulate the environment in order to isolate variables and prove cause-and-effect relationships. This chapter will backtrack a bit. There are three quantitative research designs that can fit within the action research paradigm: correlational research, causal–comparative research, and quasi-experimental research. These are described below.

CORRELATIONAL RESEARCH

Correlational research seeks to determine whether and to what degree a statistical relationship exists between two or more variables (Gay & Airasian, 2003). It is used primarily to describe an existing condition or something that has happened in the past. This means that it examines a group of people and two or more things (variables) that have already happened to them in order to determine if there is a relationship between these two things. For example, correlational research found a very strong relationship between the amount of independent reading students do outside of school and their scores on standardized achievement tests (Allington, 2001). Those students who did a great deal of reading seemed to have high scores on standardized achievement tests. Thus, there was a fairly high co-relation or correlation between these two variables. When one score went up, the other also went up and when one score went down, the other also went down.

In order to determine this correlation, researchers examined the achievement test scores of a large number of students, looked at their achievement test scores, and then looked at the amount of reading they did at home. Both of these variables (reading time and test scores) were things that had already occurred. There was no need to manipulate an environment to produce these.

Correlation Coefficient

The degree or strength of a particular correlation is measured by a correlation coefficient. A positive correlation means that when one variable increases, the other one also increases. A negative correlation means that when one variable increases, the other one decreases. A correlation coefficient of 1.00 would indicate a perfect one-to-one positive correlation. This rarely happens. A correlation coefficient of .0 means that there is absolutely no correlation between to variables. A correlation coefficient of −1.00 would indicate a perfect negative correlation. This also rarely happens.

Misusing Correlational Research

A word of warning here: Correlation does not indicate causation. Just because two variables are related, we cannot say that one causes the other. There may be other variables that have not been accounted for. In the example above, we cannot say that lots of reading causes test scores to increase, although we may suspect as much. Likewise, we cannot say that standardized achievement tests cause an increase in reading. We can say, however, that the two seem to appear together. A true experiment would then be used to isolate variables with controlled populations. However, in this case a true experiment would be unethical as you cannot deny one group of students the pleasure and benefits of reading while encouraging another.

You can find many examples in the popular media of people (usually with a political agenda) who misuse correlational research by trying to attribute cause and effect. To illustrate this misuse, note that when the water temperature goes down, far fewer people drown. An increase in water temperature correlates fairly strongly with an increase in drowning. It would be spurious to try to say that water temperature causes drowning. A variable not accounted for here, but associated to both, is that when the water temperature gets cold, people are much less likely to be swimming. Also, when the water really gets cold, it turns to ice. It is very hard to drown on an ice-covered lake. (Another misuse of correlational research is described below in the section on Whole Language in California.)

Negative Correlation

Sometimes an increase in one variable causes a decrease in another. This is an example of a negative correlation. An example of a negative correlation would be television watching and GPAs. As the amount of television watching goes up, students' GPAs go down. There is a negative correlation in that an increase in one seems to be related to a decrease in the other. Again, we cannot say that one causes the other; however, we can make predictions based on the strength of the correlation coefficient.

Making Predictions

Correlation coefficient is identified by the symbol r. When $r = 0$ to .35 the relationship between the two variables is nonexistent or low and it is useless in making predictions. When $r = .35$ to .65, there is a slight relationship. This level is useful for very limited predictions, usually with larger groups. When $r = .65$ to .85, there is a strong relationship. This would be very useful for making predictions for large groups. We could say with some certainty that an increase or decrease in one variable is related to an increase or decrease in the other. In the television example above, if r = –.75, we could reasonably predict that an increase in television would lead to a decrease in GPA. If r = –.40, we would be less confident of a prediction. A correlation coefficient of r = .86 and above shows evidence of a very strong relationship. Again, keep in mind that correlational coefficient describes the strength and direction of a relationship, not cause and effect.

CAUSAL–COMPARATIVE RESEARCH

Causal–comparative research is used to find the reason for existing differences between two or more groups (Creswell, 2002). It is used when the random assignment of participants for groups necessary for the true experiment cannot be met, which is certainly the case in most classrooms. Like correlational research, it is used to describe an existing situation. That is, it looks at conditions that have already occurred and collects data to investigate why one group is different from the other (Leedy & Ormrod, 2001). It is called causal–comparative research as it compares groups in order to find a cause for differences in measures or scores.

Like correlational research, causal–comparative research uses statistical analysis to describe conditions that already exist. However, while correlational research examines one group of participants using two or more variables, causal–comparative research examines two or more groups that differ on one or more variables. For example, if a principal was interested in looking at the effectiveness of a new math program, she could use causal–comparative research to make an informed decision. The math scores of several schools, some of which used the new program and some of which did not, would be compared and analyzed. The independent variable would be the type of math program. The dependent variable would be the average math scores on similar standardized tests from each school. If the schools using the new math program demonstrated higher test scores, and the differences in scores were statistically significant, it is reasonable to assume that the new math program may be more effective.

Whole Language in California

In California in 1996, some critics claimed that whole language approaches to reading instruction were causing reading scores to go down (McQuillan, 1998). These critics wanted all California schools to abandon whole language practices and instead adopt phonics-only reading instruction. The fallacious logic used here was that whole language approaches were being used in California schools and reading scores on standardized tests were decreasing (although this was not the case); therefore, whole language approaches must have caused the decrease in scores. Remember again that correlation does not imply causation. In this case there was a whole host of unidentified variables that may have attributed to the decrease in

FIGURE 10.1   Approaches to Reading Instruction

APPROACH TO READING INSTRUCTION	PERCENTAGE OF TEACHERS REPORTING	AVERAGE NAEP READING SCORE
Literature-based	49	221
Whole language	40	220
Phonics	11	208

standardized scores, such as an increase in class size, a decrease in funding available for school libraries, an increase in immigrant populations, and others.

Causal–comparative research was used in this situation to parse out three different groups and make comparisons. The groups consisted of fourth-grade students' scores in reading whose classroom teacher identified the primary mode of reading instruction as whole language, literature-based, or phonics. The independent variable was the type of reading instruction. The dependent variable was the average score on the NAEP standardized reading tests. The results of this research are shown in Figure 10.1.

The results show there was a difference in the groups favoring both teachers who identified their approach to reading instruction as literature-based and whole language over those teachers who identified their approach to reading instruction as phonics. Statistical analysis found that this difference was statistically significant. However, again we must be careful in how we interpret these results. This was not a true experiment in that randomized selection of participants into groups was not used. Also, there are many variables, called confounding variables, that could have accounted for the difference in scores here. For example, we have no way of knowing if the initial scores of students in each group were equal, or if the sample of classroom teachers was representative of the entire population. Also, the difference in scores could be a result of teachers versus approaches. That is, it may be that more effective teachers tend to use newer approaches such as whole language, while less effective teachers tend to use more traditional approaches. And finally, only fourth-grade teachers were surveyed here. The results may have been different if primary teachers were included.

As you can see, when reading research reports you always have to go beyond the report to look for confounding variables. What this report does conclude is that there was no evidence to support the notion that whole language causes reading test scores to decrease; however, there may be a link between literature-based and whole language instruction and positive performance on standardized reading tests.

QUASI-EXPERIMENTAL RESEARCH

The third type of research design that can be used is the quasi-experimental research design. This is the closest to the true experiment; however, in a quasi-experimental design there is no random assignment of subjects to groups. Random selection ensures that the groups being compared are relatively similar, that you are not comparing apples and oranges. As stated above, in most schools and classrooms, random selection is not possible; therefore, other ways must be used to ensure that the comparison groups are relatively similar. The two most common are pretests and matching.

In using pretests to compare groups before an investigation, simply give a test to comparison groups on the variable you are looking to examine. If they are relatively similar, you can continue with the research. If there is a significant difference between groups, there are three options: (a) find another group to compare, (b) reconfigure your existing groups so that they match, or (c) take the dissimilarity of groups into account when describing findings and conclusions.

Matching is used to create relatively similar groups. Here again a pretest is given to the entire population on the variable you are looking to examine. Based on the test results, students are matched with another who has a relatively similar score. Groups are then created by putting each person in the match in a separate group. For example, one would go in the experimental group and the other would go in the control group.

Quasi-Action Research

As you can see from the descriptions above, quasi-experimental research involves the manipulation of the environment. Thus, it has to be used with caution in an action research setting. With this type of research you are not observing an authentic classroom environment, but rather one that has been manipulated to examine a particular variable. In this sense, quasi-experimental research is also quasi-action research.

This is a good place for a reminder of what action research is: Action research is a systematic observation of one's own teaching practice. The goal is to understand what is happening in a particular classroom or school. Some types of quantitative research methodologies can be of use to this end. However, action research is not designed to prove or disprove a hypothesis, nor is it meant to provide data that can be generalized to a larger population. Quantitative methodologies in an action research project should be used simply to provide a picture of what is happening in a particular situation.

The sections below describe five different quasi-experimental designs. Figures are used to provide a clear view of the structure of each design. In these figures, Exp = experimental group, Cnt = control group, O = observation or measure, and T = treatment.

Pretest–Posttest Design

The pretest–posttest design is the most primitive quasi-experimental design. Here one group is given a pretest, a treatment, and a posttest (see Figure 10.2). Pretest and posttest scores are compared. This is often done before and after a particular

FIGURE 10.2   Pretest–Posttest Design

GROUP	TIME →		
Exp	0	T	0

unit. The variable that cannot be accounted for here is maturation. That is, simply by cognitive maturation and exposure, most students make some academic gains regardless of the technique or methodology.

Pretest–Posttest Control Group Design

This is the same as the design above except that a control group is used (see Figure 10.3). This allows the researcher to control for the variable of time and maturation. Groups can be compared based on both final scores and gain scores from pretest to posttest. There are many variables that cannot be controlled, the most significant of which is the administration of the treatment. If different teachers are teaching in the experimental and control group, it is hard to account for teaching style.

Time Series Design

Time series design examines one group over time, both before and after the treatment (see Figure 10.4). This is essentially an elaborate one-group pretest–posttest design except that here the researcher collects an extensive amount a data in order to look for patterns over time. An example of this would be a teacher who gave a

FIGURE 10.3   Pretest–Posttest Control Group Design

GROUP	TIME →		
Exp	0	T	0
Cnt	0	–	0

FIGURE 10.4   Time Series Design

GROUP	TIME →								
Exp	0	0	0	0	T	0	0	0	0

GROUP	TIME →								
Exp	T1	0	0	0	0	T2	0	0	0	0

spelling test each week for several weeks using traditional methods of spelling instruction. In the middle of the semester a new method was instituted and observations continued. Here the teacher looked for dramatic increases or decreases in spelling test scores over time.

Time Series Control Group Design

Time series control group design is the same as above except that it allows you to conduct a parallel series of observations on experimental and control groups (see Figure 10.5).

Equivalent Time-Sample Design

Using equivalent time-sample design, the treatment is sometimes present and sometimes not (see Figure 10.6). It is presented at irregular intervals; however, the measures or observations are made at regular intervals. This allows the researcher to account for and control outside influences.

THE FUNCTION OF STATISTICS

Statistical analysis can serve two functions: to describe and to infer. It is beyond the scope of this text to describe the specifics of statistical analysis; however, if you understand the concepts and limitations behind these two approaches, software

FIGURE 10.5   Time Series Control Group Design

GROUP	TIME →								
Exp	0	0	0	0	T	0	0	0	0
Cnt	0	0	0	0	–	0	0	0	0

GROUP	TIME →								
Exp	T1	0	0	0	0	T2	0	0	0	0
Cnt	T1	0	0	0	0	T1	0	0	0	0

FIGURE 10.6   Equivalent Time-Sample Design

GROUP	TIME →							
Exp	T	0	–	0	T	0	–	0

programs can be used to help you with the statistical analysis. I would also recommend the following books: *Educational Research: Competencies for Analysis and Applications* (Gay & Airasian, 2003) and *Educational Research: Planning, Conducting, and Evaluating Quantitative and Qualitative Research* (Creswell, 2002).

Descriptive Statistics

Descriptive statistics are statistical analyses used to describe an existing set of data. The most common descriptive statistical analyses are mean, mode, and median; standard deviation; and correlation coefficient. The mean is the arithmetic average of a group of scores. The mode is the single number or score that occurs most frequently in a distribution of scores. The median is the numerical center of all the data. The standard deviation tells how far apart the scores are spread from the mean. And as described above, the correlation coefficient indicates the strength of the relationship between two mean.

Inferential Statistics

Inferential statistics are statistical analyses used to determine how likely a given outcome is for an entire population based on a sample size. These analyses allow the researcher to make inferences to larger populations by collecting data on a small sample size. The most common inferential statistical analyses are the t-test, analysis of variance (ANOVA), and chi square.

The t-test is used to determine if the difference between two different means is statistically significant. Statistical significance tells us that it is very unlikely that difference in mean was caused by chance or sampling error. If the difference between two means is not statistically significant, it tells us that the differences between them are so close, we cannot say for certain whether or not it was due to chance or an error in selecting the initial sample populations. It must be pointed out also that there is a difference between statistical significance and practical significance. A difference in scores may be statistically significant; however, if this difference does not mean anything or have any practical effect, it is not practically significant. For example, there may be a statistically significant difference between two test scores, but if they both fell within the B range, there would be no practical significance between the two.

In educational research, two different levels of significance or probability are generally used: $p = .05$ and $p = .01$. A level of $p = .05$ means that we can be reasonably certain that only 5% of the differences might be due to chance or sampling error. A level of $p = .01$ means that we can be reasonably certain that only 1% of the differences might be due to chance or sampling error. Smaller sample sizes make it harder to find statistical differences and larger ones easier. For example, it is much easier to find a statistically significant difference in two groups of 3,000 than it is between two groups of 30. The t-test automatically adjusts for sample size.

While the t-test is used to compare the difference in mean between two groups, ANOVA is used to compare the difference in mean between or within three or more groups. This is a more general form of a t-test. If you want to compare frequencies within categories, a chi square is used to compare frequencies. For example, if you wanted to compare how many female and male students enjoyed a particular activity, a chi square would be used to compare the number of favorable and unfavorable responses within each gender category.

SUMMARY

- Two quantitative research designs that can be used with teacher action research projects are correlational research and causal–comparative research.
- Correlational research looks at one group to find a relationship between variables.
- Correlation coefficient describes the strength of the relationship between two variables.
- Correlation does not indicate causation.
- Predictions can be made based on the strength of the correlation coefficient.
- Causal–comparative research looks at two or more groups to compare the differences in one variable.
- Correlational research and causal–comparative research are not true experimental research designs as they do not manipulate variables or use random populations for sample groups.
- Both correlational research and causal–comparative research are used to examine existing conditions.
- Quasi-experimental design is a true experiment without random selection of participants.
- Pretests and matching are two ways to ensure groups are relatively similar before a quasi-experimental research project.
- Because quasi-experimental design manipulates an environment, it should be consider quasi-action research.
- Quasi-experimental design in action research should be used to understand a particular situation; it should not be used to prove or disprove a hypothesis or to make generalizations to a larger population.
- Descriptive statistics are used to describe a given set of data.
- Inferential statistics are used to make predictions for a general population based on a small sample size.

QUESTIONS AND ACTIVITIES

1. Find and evaluate an example of correlational research found in the popular media.
2. What are some examples of common correlations that seem to have become fact?

3. Describe three correlations that you would like to examine in a school or classroom.

4. Find an example of causal–comparative research. Identify three or more possible confounding variables.

5. Find and describe examples of quasi-experimental research. Identify three or more possible confounding variables.

DISCUSSION:
YOUR PLAN OF ACTION

Although it may not be as long as the other parts of your paper, everything in your action research report leads up to the section in which you discuss your findings and make your conclusions and recommendations based on the data collected. This is followed by what most consider to be the most important part of an action research project—your plan describing the actions you will take based on your findings. Although they are described in three separate sections here, these items do not need to appear in this order or in this exact form and may even merge in your action research report.

Also, I am making the assumption that an action research project will result in some sort of written document or report. This report may vary in length and formality depending on the purpose of your research. Even if you are doing action research simply for your own edification as a classroom teacher, I would encourage you to create a short written document of your findings and describe ideas for change. Writing helps to clarify and organize your thinking and enables you to see patterns or associations you may have missed. Also, a written report documents your professional development. In most states teachers periodically have to engage in some kind of continuing education to maintain their teaching license. An action research report can be used for this purpose. Finally, having a written account of your findings and ideas allows you to share them with others, either in oral or written form. In this way you can help to keep the field of education evolving and moving forward.

CONCLUSIONS AND RECOMMENDATIONS

A conclusion is a reasoned deduction. That is, you come to believe one thing based on another thing or series of things. Based on the data you have collected and reported, what does it all mean? What is it that you now know to be true? What can we deduce from the data you have presented? Your conclusion is often no more than a paragraph or two describing your current state of knowing or a list of things you have come to believe as a result of your study.

A recommendation is a general suggestion for what is believed to be an effective choice or action based on your findings. You tell how your findings might be used or provide advice as to what should be done differently. Keep in mind, however, that the line between conclusions and recommendations is often blurred. Some action research papers only have conclusions; others only have recommendations. Still others, like those described next, have a combination of both.

Jo Henriksen, St. Louis Park, Minnesota

Jo Henriksen is a gifted-education teacher at Peter Hobart Elementary and Aquila Primary Center in St. Louis Park, Minnesota. Instead of the traditional parent–teacher conference, she studied student-led conferences involving identified gifted students in grades 1 through 3. Before their conferences, students were asked to synthesize and describe in writing their learning during the quarter. This information was shared with parents during the conference.

Jo's goals in this action research were to understand fully the process of student-led conferences and to see whether they were beneficial and worth continuing. To collect data, she created a survey for students (see Figure 11.1). And because she was conducting the conferences, she was able to record her thoughts and impressions following each conference. She created a checklist to guide her reflections (see Figure 11.2).

In the checklists in Figures 11.1 and 11.2, Jo Henriksen defined specific behaviors or attributes. The checklist allowed her to focus on these attributes consistently

---

FIGURE 11.1   Student Survey Form

Name: _____   Grade: _____   Today's Date: _____

HOW DID YOUR CONFERENCE GO?

1. Who came to your conference besides you?	mom	dad	both
2. Were you glad you could come to your conference?	yes	no	not sure
3. Do you think your parents learned more about what you are doing in class?	yes	no	not sure
4. Did you learn more about putting facts into categories?	yes	no	not sure
5. Did you get to talk enough?	yes	no	not sure
6. Was the time long enough for the conference?	yes	no	not sure

7. What is the best part of getting to come to your own conference?

8. Could anything make the conference better next time?

FIGURE 11.2   Teacher Reflection Form

Name: _____   Grade: _____   Today's Date: _____

REFLECTIONS ON THE CHILD-LED CONFERENCE

1. Who came to the conference?	mom	dad	both
2. Was the tone of the conference pleasant?	yes	no	comments:
3. Did parents seem to learn more about what happens in class?	yes	no	comments:
4. Did the child handle the vocabulary of the categorizing exercise?	yes	no	comments:
5. Did the child handle the categorizing exercise?	yes	no	comments:
6. Did the child get to talk enough?	yes	no	comments:
7. Was the time long enough for the conference?	yes	no	comments:

8. Do any points need to be remembered because of this conference?

9. Do you need to schedule another appointment for a conference without the child? Topic?

---

with each student. After presenting the data in her report, Jo wrote the following conclusion.

Conclusions

I came to the following conclusions regarding student-led conferences:

1. They were a wonderful opportunity to meet with children in a pleasant situation.
2. Children learned more about what they have learned, thanks to this form of conferencing.
3. The conferences were energizing as opposed to energy draining.
4. Our district schedules the Fall conferences very early. Since my Gifted Education program doesn't start until the second full week of school, I barely have time to get much work done with the children before it is conference time. I am going to have to do some thinking about the tightness of the schedule.
5. I will do more preconference planning with each child before the big night.
6. I routinely have a family night each spring. This is an opportunity for all to see what students have produced. I am thinking that I will have this

night prior to spring conferences. That way less time will be needed at conferences to explain the projects. More time can be devoted to discussion and assessment of projects.

7. Whereas I can't insist that parents schedule conferences, I am really determined to have conferences with virtually 100% of my students.

8. The conferences will still be only 25 minutes in length. Many of my students, being who they are, love to talk much and at length. I will have to think about how to reconcile the time allotment to still satisfy the desire of these children, if possible.

9. I absolutely will continue the practice.

Final Thoughts

Overall, I would have to say that my decision to conduct student-led conferences was good. I have worked in gifted education for 9 years, in regular education a lot longer. I know what makes children happy a lot of the time and what helps parents to feel secure some of the time. I also know what helps me to maintain zest for the job that I do. I designed the conferences to meet the needs of my students and families. I also designed the conferences to be a tool to help me to be more effective in my position. Conferences are an inherently difficult time for me; however, I look forward to making this time more positive and productive through the use of student-led conferences.

Cathy Stamps, Fifth Grade, Hopkins Elementary School

Cathy Stamps was interested in finding out if her fifth-grade students learned better when they sat by their friends or when she assigned them seats. She collected data by (a) taking field notes focusing specifically on students' behavior, attitude, and production; (b) comparing samples of students' work that were completed in both settings; and (c) administering a student survey. She made the following conclusions and recommendations:

Based on my observations and student responses, I would conclude that learning is positively affected when students have a say in where they sit. They feel more ownership in their learning; therefore, they are more excited about learning. I know when I am at conferences or workshops, I would much rather have my choice of people to work with versus being told who to work with. I think the saying, "Treat others the way you would like to be treated" applies to this situation. By giving students a chance to self-assign themselves, they wasted less time working out differences that often hinder them when trying to complete a task in a minimal amount of time.

My experience with this investigation has been beneficial. Students knew what was expected and also knew the consequences if they couldn't handle working in self-assigned groups. However, I did assign seats periodically in order to mix up the class and decrease cliques.

EVALUATION OF THE STUDY

There is no such thing as the perfect study. After reporting conclusions and recommendations, some researchers like to evaluate the effectiveness of their study, explain particular aspects of it, or describe how they might do it differently the next time.

Jim Vavreck, St. Peter, Minnesota

Jim conducted a study to see how his sixth-grade students perceived intelligence and creativity. Data were collected by using a questionnaire and a self-rating scale (see Figures 11.3 and 11.4). Jim evaluated his study as he reported the data. He did a nice job of letting us inside his head as he wrestled with various parts of his study. You can also see him thinking as a researcher in that every question answered seemed to result in another question asked. I have included an excerpt:

> The students in this study generally seemed to feel that either creativity or intelligence was a personal strength. Only 13% rated their intelligence and creativity as equal. A follow-up question regarding what evidence each student could give for his or her personal ratings in intelligence and creativity would be helpful in identifying how students are differentiating between creativity and intelligence as they rate themselves in each.
>
> **Other Implications**
>
> It appears that I should have described the rating scale more clearly. It seems that either this group is exceptionally above average or else they did not understand the concept of average. On the other hand, perhaps they

FIGURE 11.3   Student Survey

Name: _____

1. What is intelligence?
2. What is creativity?
3. How are intelligence and creativity related?
4. Is it possible to be creative without being intelligent?
5. Is it possible to be intelligent without being creative?

FIGURE 11.4   Student Self-Rating Scale

Name: _____

1. How creative are you on a scale of 0–10 where 5 is average?
2. How intelligent are you on a scale of 0–10 where 5 is average?

have a good, albeit unrealistic, self-concept. Or maybe they pictured extremely low students to compare themselves with.

I am also interested in exploring the differences in how the girls rated themselves and how the boys did using a much larger sample. The current indication is that the girls rated themselves higher in intelligence and creativity. A longitudinal study could be done to see if the self-ratings in creativity and intelligence change over time.

DESIGNING A NEW PLAN OR PROGRAM

Designing a new plan or program is putting the action in action research. That means you have to do something or make a plan to do something. In some rare instances the results of an action research project will indicate that everything is just fine, in which case your action research plan is a plan to do nothing. However, most action research projects result in one of five possible outcomes:

1. *Greater understanding of the situation, child, or students in general.* In this case, you should describe how your interactions or instruction will change to reflect this greater understanding.

2. *The discovery of a problem.* Finding and defining a problem are the initial elements of the problem-solving process. If your action research project results in the discovery of a problem, use the problem-solving strategies described in Chapter 4 to create a plan of action. Once a plan has been created, it can be implemented and evaluated. This calls for another action research project, and thus, action research becomes a vehicle for the continued growth and evolution of a classroom or school.

3. *A plan, program, or pedagogical method is found to be effective.* An action research report would describe why and how it is effective and allow you to make a case for its continued use. Also, even in an effective plan, program, or pedagogical method, some elements can be made more effective. Your research report should identify these.

4. *A plan, program, or pedagogical method is found to need modification.* Any new plan on paper rarely results in its perfect functioning in reality. Having to adjust and adapt is a normal part of doing anything new or innovative. An action research report is used in this situation to identify the elements that need to be modified and to describe how they will be changed.

5. *A plan, program, or pedagogical method is found to be ineffective.* Action research can be used to document the ineffectiveness of a program. Your research report can be used to support the change or elimination of the plan, program, or pedagogical method.

Creating a New Plan or Program

Sometimes as a result of your action research, you need to design or create a new plan or program. You will likely be more successful if the new plan or program contains the following three elements: (a) a school philosophy or mission statement, (b) goals, and (c) a rationale.

School Philosophy or Mission Statement.   Each school or school district should have a school philosophy, a mission statement, or sometimes both. Putting this at the top of any new plan helps you align your objectives with the school's and provides support and justification for the ideas that follow.

A school philosophy is the general belief, policy, or set of ideas formulated by the educational system that reflects the values of the school and community. This may describe the nature of learning or how education and learning fit in a broader scheme of human endeavors. Consider the following example:

> The Anytown School District is a cooperative, democratic venture between students, parents, teachers, and community. It shall be the policy of this district to maintain the highest academic standards, to engage in the best practices in education, and to enable every child to reach his or her full potential.

Thus stated, the school philosophy can be used to support plans that would help maintain high academic standards, such as smaller class sizes, increased teacher development activities, or more books and computers in the classrooms. It can be used to justify change when current practices do not reflect what research describes as the best practices in teaching, such as when schools engage in an over-reliance on standardized tests to describe learning or educational progress. It also can be used to support new programs or the reallocation of resources when certain students are not able to reach their full potential, such as those with special learning needs, the intellectually gifted and highly creative, students with physical disabilities, and those from minority cultures. Thus, a school's philosophy can be used as an agent of change and continued growth.

A mission statement states what the school is trying to accomplish in a very general sense. Consider the following example:

The purpose of our education system is to help learners acquire the knowledge and skills necessary to become constructive world citizens, informed decision makers, and lifelong learners.

The mission statement is sometimes combined with or incorporated into the school philosophy. If your proposed plan or program meets resistance by colleagues, a building principal, or a school board, a mission statement can be used to justify or support what you want to implement.

Goals.   Goals define what you hope to accomplish with your new plan or program. They also help you in evaluation. That is, to determine success, you judge whether you have met some or all of your goals. Goals also help keep your plan focused and prevent you from wandering off into unrelated areas. Again, you can create a better case for your new plan or program if your goals are aligned with the school philosophy and mission statement.

Rationale.   The rationale explains why the goals are important. You describe the benefit to the learner, the school, or society in general. Sometimes it helps to put your goals in a theoretical context.

A Less Formal Plan of Action

Again, depending on the nature and purpose of your action research project, sometimes it is appropriate to have an informal plan of action. This may be a simple description of your intentions or a list of specific steps that you plan to take. Action research is built on the premise that some type of action will result from your research. The final measure of your action research is the degree to which it clearly asks and answers your question, communicates your ideas, and serves to promote positive change.

A final word: I want to reiterate that the items described in this chapter should be adapted to your particular situation to meet the needs of your research project.

SUMMARY

- The final part of an action research report is making conclusions and recommendations, evaluating the study, and making a plan of action.
- A conclusion is a reasoned deduction based on your findings.
- A recommendation is a general suggestion for change based on your findings.
- An evaluation assesses the general effectiveness of your study and explains any interesting or important elements of it.
- A plan of action describes exactly what you intend to do as a result of your action research.

- Action research should result in some form of written document or report, which varies in length and formality.
- A new plan or program is more apt to be successfully implemented if it includes a philosophy or mission statement, goals, and a rationale.

QUESTIONS AND ACTIVITIES

1. Read your school district's philosophy or mission statement or use that of another school district. Do you agree with it? What would you include or eliminate? Can you find an instance in which practice does not align with this philosophy or mission statement?
2. Create your own philosophy or mission statement for your school district and for your classroom.
3. Find a plan, program, or piece of curriculum. Identify the goals. Do the goals align with the mission statement and rationale?
4. Describe a change you would like to see. Use your district's philosophy or mission statement to support your ideas.
5. Describe a class or a particular subject area. List three to eight general goals for that class or subject area. Provide a rationale for their importance.
6. Use the excerpts of one of the studies presented in this chapter to create a plan of action.

SECTION III

SAMPLES

CHAPTER TWELVE

SAMPLE ACTION RESEARCH PROJECTS

This chapter contains seven short action research projects along with my comments. Most of these action research projects do not contain a literature review. Although the literature review adds an important dimension that connects your ideas to the literature, it is not always a necessary element.

SAMPLE 12.1

ALISON REYNOLDS, MINNEAPOLIS, MINNESOTA

Few action research projects have touched me as much as the one written by Alison Reynolds. She demonstrated how the domains of art and science might sometimes overlap. Indeed, both are ways of seeing and representing reality. Alison examined a small part of her world and brought it to life. She used words as an artist uses paint to create a picture on the canvas of our minds.

When Alison started this action research project, she was overwhelmed by the large quantity of data. She wanted us to understand the environment in which she worked but did not know where to start. She solved her dilemma by focusing on one student. You can see in her poignant picture a portrayal of the human spirit and an understanding of her teaching environment.

THE PAINTER

Sammy

There is a way that he comes into the classroom that is similar to the way that a storm blows into town. It is something akin to a little breeze that follows him through the doorway. By the end of class the furniture often lays toppled from his winds. At 12 years of age his anger is profound. He is verbally confrontational and is often "up in your face." Everyone is a "bitch" to him; he uses "fat ass" for men, "whore" and "slut" for women, and "fish" for girls his age.

Sammy has been at Greenwood Treatment School for 2 years. Greenwood School is one step above residential treatment. It is populated by students who have been unable to benefit from a slew of public schools throughout the Twin Cities area.

Sammy is a large boy weighing about 175 pounds. He possesses an artistic nature. Although he uses profanity for his daily interactions now, the rhythm of his speech often sounds a little delayed and awkward. It is as if he is not quite comfortable with this new persona of his. He acts like a tough guy that still has to think about his lines before saying them. His rage is real though. The expression of that rage is awkward and violent, but there is water in that well.

At School

When Sammy started at Greenwood School 2 years ago he was rambunctious, followed the classroom jokers, and did more fooling around than anything else. He was not verbally confrontational. He was not assaultive. He was not violent. Naturally, he did have conflicts with other students, but these conflicts had a different tone to them. They were conflicts about small student disputes such as taking someone else's chair, grabbing someone's pencil, or having a little too much fun at the expense of another.

Sammy was in the fifth grade when he started at Greenwood School, but his academic level was in the third- to fourth-grade range. I first met him because he started coming to my classroom to get his academic skills caught up. I had suggested to his fifth-grade teacher that because of Sammy's academic delays, he might be better served in a lower level classroom. I was working in a third/fourth-grade classroom at the time.

I worked with Sammy for a year and a half to try and get him caught up with his peers. He applied himself to learning addition, subtraction, and multiplication. He completed simple writing assignments. He read as many second- and third-grade-level books as possible in a given class period. At the end of each class, Sammy could see the math that he did, the writing that he completed, and the stack of books that he had read.

The purpose of him doing all this work was not only to help him catch up academically with his peers, but also to provide him with a visual pile at the end of every class that he could look at and say, "I did this much today." Helping Sammy to build his confidence relating to his academics was as important as his acquisition of academic skills. He became very focused on completing his work, often ignoring other classroom disruptions. He also became less vulnerable to the criticism of his fifth-grade peers.

Painting

It was during this period that Sammy started painting watercolor pictures. He would title each one the same: A Sunny Day. Because he would give these pictures to me, I acquired a large collection of Sammy's artwork.

I learned much about Sammy because he talked a great deal to me. He told me about his impoverished home life. He spoke about the violence in his neighborhood. He described the struggles of his family members. His father had come to "the States" from Mexico. His mother was African American. He had a 20-year-old brother in prison. He had an 18-year-old brother who was getting ready to marry his pregnant girlfriend. Sammy understood that his life and the lives of those in his family had troubles, but the troubles had not possessed his spirit and heart.

The Zoo

One day our school went to the Minnesota Zoo. Many of the students were doing tough guy clowning with each other while walking around the grounds. I broke off from the main group with a smaller group of these students. Sammy was with us. As we were walking, running, and bumping into each other, there on a grassy knoll was a flock of baby ducklings with their mother.

Sammy stood and watched the ducks for a long moment. Then he spotted an older duck approaching the group of ducklings. Sammy took off running after that duck. He chased it all over the grassy lawn, around trees and bushes. He never caught the duck, but if he had I am sure that it would have been safe in his care. He was still at that child's age where he would chase and capture something because of its freedom, and then tenderly care for what he had caught.

Life

On the Tuesday following the school's trip to the zoo, Sammy came to school, but, I did not see him the entire day. The following day the same thing happened. I spoke with the school's therapy staff to ask why Sammy had come to school but was not participating in class or other activities.

Sammy's brother, the one who had been preparing to marry his pregnant girlfriend, had been killed. Sammy was at home on a Sunday evening and heard somebody knocking at the door. Sammy opened the door and saw his brother laying on his stomach with a trail of blood behind him. His brother had been shot and had crawled on his stomach up to his home. He died at the doorway.

Sammy's heart turned that night. He became the embodiment of his family's troubles. It is common to hear him banging against the lockers in the hall, yelling at the top of his lungs. The therapy staff working with him stated that they were trying to help Sammy find more appropriate ways of dealing with his anger.

Surprisingly, about 2 months after the murder of Sammy's brother, students at school started to use that tragedy and loss as a means of getting to Sammy. They made fun of him for having a brother who had been murdered.

Life at School

I don't see Sammy as much as I used to. He mostly stays with his sixth-grade classmates. When I do see him, it is only to talk. We speak about how someone who has "passed" lives on in the hearts of those who were close to him. We speak about how to use the death of someone close to you to make you a stronger person on this earth. Periodically we speak about education and opportunity. When someone interrupts these conversations, Sammy immediately switches back into his aggressive and proving new self. I, along with everyone else, become the "bitch."

I don't expect to receive "A Sunny Day" picture ever again. Summer has passed for him. Yet, I know that he still holds a paintbrush in a hand behind his back. I don't know what his new pictures will look like. I don't know what will happen to him. I do know that if a student loses faith and strength in his soul, you lose the ability to teach him.

The desired action in the case of Sammy is a call for understanding. Alison enables us to see a human face and real-life problems behind the statistics and test scores.

SAMPLE 12.2
KAY DICKE, EDEN PRAIRIE

Kay Dicke created a nice, crisp introduction that gets the reader right into the paper. Her descriptions are precise, allowing us to see exactly what is happening at each stage.

MOTIVATING STUDENTS TO READ

Reading is an important part of a child's education. All subjects at any grade level include reading in many forms, whether it's nonfiction or a classic piece of fictional literature. There are many children who enjoy reading, but there are also many who do not. The benefits of reading are limitless, but what can be done to motivate all students to increase their time spent reading?

Action Research Question: How can I motivate my sixth-grade students to increase their time spent reading?

Methods of Collecting Data

Collecting data was the first step of the action research process. The first method utilized was a general reading survey given to 27 sixth-grade students. Questions asked pertained to the amount of free time out of school students spent reading and the types of books they read. Results of the survey showed that the majority of students like to read but most spent very little time outside of school doing it, usually 1 to 3 hours each week. Of the books read, adventure and humorous books were by far the most popular genres selected. The survey results supported a need for increased reading by these sixth-grade students.

The next step of the research process was to begin observing and taking daily field notes during a 1-week period. These observations took place throughout the day during a variety of different subjects. Many questions from the student survey were considered as these observations were made, including: How often did students read during the school day? What types of reading did they do? What kinds of books do they select to read during their free reading time? What can be done to promote more reading by all students? Are students choosing books that are appropriate for their reading abilities?

Observations lead to some general conclusions: Several students were observed reading and making great progress by completing one or more books throughout the week. At least seven students really did not seem to take an interest in the books they selected and spent more time looking around the classroom. Others had a different book each day, not actually reading one book completely. Students interested in reading often chose to read after completing assignments in class. There was definitely a wide variety of readers in this group.

From my field notes a checklist was created [see Figure 12.1]. Each day for 1 week during silent reading time a small group of four or five students was observed. The checklist was used to look for the following behaviors: being on task, progress completing the same book, and the type of book being read. The checklist was an easy and useful method of collecting specific data.

FIGURE 12.1 Independent Reading Checklist

STUDENT	DATE	TIME	TYPE OF BOOK	ON TASK	COMMENTS

After 2 weeks of collecting field notes and using my checklist, I asked students to begin using a log sheet to record the number of minutes and the genre of books read over a 2-week period both at home and at school. The number of minutes was totaled and written on a chart to track their progress.

Findings

Students responded positively to the reading log at school. They were very dedicated about tracking their minutes. As the study progressed, they took on more responsibility with their reading and began to make sure to track minutes spent reading their social studies book and other expository reading material encountered throughout the day.

At first, the number of minutes read at home was not as high as at school. Many students had very poor results here and quite a few did not return the log sheet from home. However, the minutes read at school and home were documented and would be used as a baseline to measure progress.

A high percentage of sixth-grade students seemed to pick up on the importance of reading through their logs. A chart was posted in the classroom where their minutes of reading were tracked. Many students compared their minutes to others and seemed pleased with their results. They were always eager to get a new reading log sheet. Also, positive comments were made by parents at conferences. Here, goals were set to improve the time spent reading at home in order to increase students' total minutes.

The next log sheets were given for an additional 2 weeks. Again, these students took real initiative in tracking their reading minutes at school. However, the results of the home log were just as poor as the last time. Many still did not turn them in or if they did, they did little reading. However, 80% of the students in this class did improve their total minutes of reading (in school and at home) from the first reading log.

I realized that I needed to take more time discussing my expectations for the home logs. I talked with students and found that they read a lot of things at home such as web pages on the Internet, magazines, and even cereal boxes. I encouraged them to log those minutes and helped them to realize that they were reading more than they thought.

The results of the third reading log were improved again: 92% of the home logs were returned this time and the number of total minutes read (in school and at home) was increased.

Conclusions

Students took pride in their accomplishments here and at the same time, they found that reading can be something enjoyable to do every day. Small gains were made in the amount of reading time. By the end of the school year my ultimate goal would be to get all students reading more and reading more independently without instruction.

SAMPLE 12.3
LOUANN STRACHOTA

LouAnn Strachota, a paraprofessional working in a classroom, was in the process of getting her teacher certification. I included her work to show how preservice teachers might use action research to analyze and reflect on their learning environments. LouAnn wanted to study the behavior of students in one of her classes; however, she did not know where to start. This is a common predicament among beginning action researchers. To provide more focus, she did a short pilot study to see what behaviors students were displaying. She used this initial observation to create a checklist (see Figure 12.2). Then, instead of trying to chart every student's behavior, she decided to look at one student each day. This made the task more manageable and helped her focus on specific behaviors over a predetermined time.

ON- AND OFF-TASK BEHAVIOR IN A HIGH SCHOOL HEALTH CLASS

This study was undertaken in order to examine the relationship between on- and off-task behavior in an Emotional Behavior Disorder (EBD) level 4 resource room in a high school health class. I work as a paraprofessional here and am in the process of getting my teaching certification. I was interested in finding out why there were differences in students' on- and off-task behaviors.

FIGURE 12.2   On-Task Behavior Checklist

Student's Name: <u>Don N.</u>   Date: _____

Recorded at 5-minute intervals.

ON-TASK BEHAVIOR. THE STUDENT IS:	10:30	10:35	10:40	10:45	10:50	10:55	11:00
—Working							
—Listening to directions		x		x	x		
—Reading			x				
—Engaged in listening	x						
—Working with somebody else							
—Responding to the teacher							
—Other							

Collecting Data

Data were collected from observations using a checklist that indicated on- and off-task behavior at 5-minute intervals [Figures 12.2 and 12.3].

This health class was taught from 10:17 A.M. to 11:12 A.M. 5 days a week. I chose to study students' behavior in this particular class because there were only four students here: three boys and one girl. One of these students was observed each day over the course of 17 school days. The behavior of each student was noted at 5-minute intervals.

The first few times that students were told that they were going to be observed they kept watching to see what marks they were being given. After a few days, however, the stigma of being observed wore off and they acted in their usual manner.

The Classroom Setting

This EBD classroom contained 10 chair-desks placed in a half-circle surrounding a kidney-shaped table in front of the room. There were three study carrels in the back of the room and a teacher's desk in the front of the room on the far left side. Rules regarding behavior were posted on a chart in front of the room. The study carrels were used for students who displayed disruptive or inappropriate behaviors. If there were additional infractions, students were sent to an independent study room.

FIGURE 12.3   Off-Task Behavior Checklist

Recorded at 5-minute intervals.

OFF-TASK BEHAVIOR. THE STUDENT IS:	10:30	10:35	10:40	10:45	10:50	10:55	11:00
—Talking to somebody						x	x
—Doodling							
—Listening to another student							
—Looking in his/her desk							
—In a study carrel							
—Working on something else							
—Making noises							
—Walking around							
—Other							

OBSERVATIONS:

Don has not been to class for a few days—but while here he was working very well until the last 10 minutes of class. He then walked around the room and talked to other students in the room.

Other behavior management techniques included three forms of classroom contracts: limited, expected, and privileged. Each contract had varying levels of student privileges.

Findings

One noticeable observation was that students had a hard time staying focused around 11:00 A.M. because they were hungry. Students started watching the clock around this time, waiting for the bell to ring. Included here are the observations for each student [see Table 12.1].

Don

Don was observed only twice due to low attendance. When others were working on assignments, Don seemed to work well and stay on task. During the last 10 minutes of class he usually talked to other students.

Sally

Sally was observed four times. She seemed to spend most of her time working with an aide. She missed 3 days of class during this observation. When she returned, she worked hard to catch up on her assignments.

TABLE 12.1   Total On-Task and Off-Task Behaviors

STUDENT	ON-TASK BEHAVIOR	OFF-TASK BEHAVIOR
Don	85%	15%
Sally	90%	10%
Tom	80%	20%
Harry	83%	17%
Total average	84.5%	15.5%

Tom

Tom was observed four times. He came every day but sometimes had to leave early to prepare for a choir concert that he was in. One day he was the only student in class and was able to work without distraction and stay on task. However, if somebody else was talking, Tom became easily distracted. When Sally was in the room, he often wanted to talk with her. He told another student that he had a crush on her. He was asked several times by the teacher or aide to stop talking. When Sally was not in class, Tom's on-task behavior improved by 15%. Tom is a good student and can work very well in class when he wants to. However, it appears that he is easily distracted by Sally.

Harry

Harry was observed six times. His lowest percentage for on-task behavior was 40% and his highest was 100%. On his low day, Harry complained about being extremely tired and said he was not going to do any work. My observations also showed that he did not stay on task very well when he was tired. When he was tired, he complained that he was not feeling well and said he wanted to lie on the floor. If Harry appeared to be in a good mood, he worked very well and stayed on task. Harry also stayed on task much better if there was only one other student in class.

Conclusions

The high percentage of on-task behavior could be contributed to the small class size. My observations showed that when fewer students were in class they spent more time working. Also, students completed all assignments and stayed on task when they were working directly with the teacher or with me.

Off-task behavior resulted most often when (a) students were moody or tired, (b) students finished their assignments early and disrupted others,

(c) there were more students in the class, and (d) one student liked another and preferred talking to work.

Recommendations

Based on these observations, I recommend the following:

1. Students should have something else to work on or read when they are finished with their work. They need preplanned assignments and other things to do to keep them occupied.

2. Students should be separated from other students if they keep talking.

3. Assignments should involve opportunities for hands-on experiences and allow students to interact. This would keep them involved and prevent boredom.

4. The units should be made more interesting by using content enrichment activities that keep students involved.

Things That Worked

These are some of the things that seemed to work in this health class:

1. Students recorded their ideas of what was interesting or important in each chapter (instead of using a study guide or worksheet).

2. A bingo game was created with the vocabulary words from each chapter.

3. Teams were used and a quiz game was created that used questions from the assigned chapters.

4. A visual organizer that showed the content covered during the unit seemed to help students understand.

Final Thought

Overall, I feel that a variety of methods should be incorporated into the curriculum to keep EBD students on task and interested in the subjects being taught.

SAMPLE 12.4
GEORGINA L. PETE

Georgina's action research project reads very much like a staffing report (which it was). At the end of this report she outlines four things that she will try to implement to improve the situation.

HELPING BRANDON

Being the new Talented and Gifted (TAG) teacher in a suburban school district in the Twin Cities metro area, I had high hopes of starting the year off with a bang. However, I was approached not long after the school year started by a fourth-grade teacher who had threatened one of her students with being taken out of the TAG program because of his low grades in her classroom. I decided this was an issue I needed to become involved with. This is a summary of the information I collected and the recommendations made for this student.

Data Collection

Information collected for this research was in the form of conferencing, observations with field notes, and interviewing. All data were collected over a 4-week period between the months of October and November.

The Conference

The first step was to set up a conference with the classroom teacher (Ms. Lee) and the principal (Ms. Kelly). Ms. Kelly was very familiar with this student, who I will refer to as Brandon, as she had him in her office several times to deal with discipline problems. In fact, she said that he had the most discipline offences in the school. Ms. Kelly printed out a list of his infractions. These had to do mostly with being disrespectful and physical aggression.

The conference was very informative. Brandon's behavior in class, on the bus, and during recess was not what I saw when he was in my TAG classroom. I knew him to be polite, excited about learning, humorous, and well liked by his peers. Ms. Lee painted quite a different picture. She thought of him as very disrespectful and said he was not cutting it with his classroom assignments (he was not turning them in). Since he was not showing her his giftedness she felt he should not have the privilege of leaving the regular education classroom to go to the TAG classroom.

Ms. Kelly played a key role in this conference. She was very concerned about Brandon's future, as was I. She felt that the TAG classroom was something very important to him. Here he felt like he had some power and importance. She cautioned that taking away his TAG classes might make this troubled boy's situation more disastrous. I agreed.

We all agreed that something needed to be done to help Brandon steer his school career in a positive direction. His test scores indicated that he should have been operating at a much higher level; however, he was getting C's and D's in his classes. I agreed to make observations of him in the classroom and on the playground to see what might be done. The teacher and principal were going to stay in close contact with Brandon's mother (the father did not seem to play an active role in his son's education). All agreed that the mother needed to play a more active role in Brandon's education and help out with any action plan.

Observations

Brandon could be very sneaky and dishonest. He would look you in the eye and tell you he had all his work done when he did not. When I observed him in the classroom he seemed to have a high level of on-task behavior if he was working with a partner in a situation where both needed to cooperate in order to get the assignment done. However, when working by himself, he did not use his time very efficiently and became a distraction to others with his silliness. He also did not seem to put a great deal of effort into his assignments. Ms. Lee said that in the past, Brandon had claimed to have lost missing assignments or left them at home.

I also observed Ms. Lee to be very negative. In every discussion that I had with her, she never said one positive comment about him, while Ms. Kelly had made several positive comments and expressed concern for his future and seemed to have a real interest in turning his situation around.

Interviews

I interviewed Brandon and three of his peers in his TAG group. This gave me the impression that he has a history of being unorganized and irresponsible. They all agreed that they would not like to have Brandon in charge of getting something done for a group activity because "he never gets anything done." However, all looked favorably at him as a friend and seemed to enjoy working with him in TAG classes. They especially liked listening to him discuss and tell stories.

Brandon agreed that he needed to work hard in school at being more focused on his responsibilities. His attempts to be better organized and more responsible with his assignments usually lasted only a day at the most.

Recommendations

Based on the information collected here, I recommend the following:

1. Brandon should be placed in a different classroom. His mother also made this request, which Ms. Kelly granted. I believe that both the mother and Ms. Kelly felt as I did, that Ms. Lee was not a positive influence on Brandon and he would be better matched with another teacher.

2. I will check in with Brandon on a regular basis. He is a very social person and likes an audience. I think that given an opportunity to express himself in an appropriate manner with somebody who is not continually pushing to complete his homework with a higher quality, Brandon might feel less of an urge to act out by being silly in class and causing distraction. My goal here will be to encourage quality effort.

3. Communication with Brandon's mother must improve. He should get some positive calls home when he makes progress. His mother is used to getting calls home about discipline and late assignments, but not for positive behavior. I will be responsible for contacting her when Brandon and I have made some breakthroughs.

4. Brandon and his family should work on his organizational skills. I will recommend some reading for him and his family along this line.

Conclusions

I am hopeful that Brandon will benefit from these recommendations. I find him to be a very pleasant boy, but also someone who could end up being a leader in a negative way. I feel confident that he will enjoy having my interest in him where he can express himself freely. He will be helped in all areas by a strong commitment at home to quality and organization.

SAMPLE 12.5
TERESA VAN BATAVIA, EISENHOWER ELEMENTARY, HOPKINS, MINNESOTA

Teresa Van Batavia's research shows the work of a master teacher carefully observing her students and making decisions based on students' needs. In this report she is able to create a good sense of being there. As you read the notes from her writing conferences, this classroom comes to life. Suddenly you can see exactly where her students are as writers. She also takes us inside her head, letting us overhear her thinking as she processes the information and makes decisions based on that information.

WRITING WORKSHOP

My first-grade students at Eisenhower Elementary are involved in a writer's workshop setting at least three times a week. My concern is that children may be slipping through the cracks—doing little or no writing and not being noticed.

Data Collection

The first form of data collection that I used is that of a weekly checklist. As I circulated among students during the 2-week period from November 15 through December 3, 1999, I carried a clipboard and checked off each type of writing activity that I observed [see Figure 12.4]. This checklist became an effective tool for helping me to choose mini-lesson topics for the children. I will continue to use this on an informal basis throughout the year.

FIGURE 12.4   Writer's Workshop Checklist

Writer's Workshop Checklist, Week of November 15–19, 1999

Generating/prewriting	~~HHT~~ ~~HHT~~	
Drawing/sketching	~~HHT~~ |||
Drafting	~~HHT~~ ~~HHT~~ ~~HHT~~ ~~HHT~~ ~~HHT~~ ~~HHT~~	
Revising	~~HHT~~	
Editing	|||
Conference/talking		
Reading		
Other	~~HHT~~ ||

In addition to the checklists, I met individually with each student and also collected their writing folders for further study of their writing habits. Following are my notes of these conferences.

Conference Notes—Individual Students

Joni is most comfortable starting with an illustration and then writing one or two sentences to accompany the picture. Her latest effort, however, is a story inspired by her neighbor's car accident. She is struggling with understanding how to expand it beyond two sentences.

Lynn and Valerie have regularly referred to their topic list and have created two to three stories each. Their writings have a solid beginning, middle, and end.

Tony, Walter, Jason, William, and Sonjia have accomplished very little over the past 2 months. Their folders contain very primitive drawings. All four students described frustration in choosing an idea and drawing or writing about it. Brainstorming ideas together failed to elicit a solid topic for which any of the four were willing to write about.

Tim has worked feverishly for the past five writing sessions on a story about his broken arm. He has included a great deal of detail on his surroundings as well as his emotions at the time.

Publishing has become Ryan's frantic goal. He worked diligently on a story titled "My World," a hodgepodge of facts and opinions about the world around him. We revised and edited together and now he is ready for publication.

Becky and Cassandra, two highly able students, have made little progress. The contents of their folders are simple drawings with little depth in writing.

Brian, Nancy, and Kirsten have successfully used the Five W's Web (who, what, where, why, and when) to generate ideas for their stories. They made a smooth transition from web to rough draft. All three found the web to be a useful tool and plan to use it again.

Picture books are the focus for Heather and Alicia as they sketch and then add the text to their drawings.

Unable to fathom the fact that he may choose topics for himself, Mitchell fluctuates between drawing and finding me to ask if his topic choice is acceptable. He is able to construct a very creative, oral story. These stories lose a lot in the recording process, which is difficult for Mitchell.

Conference Notes—Writing Difficulties

Two boys in my class are plagued by a need to spell each and every word perfectly. They are reluctant to put anything in writing without first verifying with an adult. This has had an adverse effect on the quality of their thoughts.

Another child has very poor fine-motor skills and several speech difficulties. He has been unable to function in this setting without an adult close by his side.

Conclusions

The two forms of data collection that I used supported each other in pointing out that I have a wide variety of stages of the writing process occurring on a daily basis. First of all, as I feared, five of my struggling students were frequently off task, frustrated by writer's block, unable to come up with a topic (even from their personal topic lists), and unable to sustain a 15–20 minute work period. As a result, I will begin a series of short mini-lessons with this small group. These lessons will begin with topic selection. This group of students seems to need a very step-by-step introduction and guided tour through the stages of the writing process. It will be necessary to bring them from start to finish through the entire process in a more structured setting.

I found the majority of my students to be in the drafting stage of their writing. These students varied widely in ability, but were similar in the fact that they could remain focused on their writing for a longer period of time than the three struggling writers mentioned above. Seven of my students created a Five W's Web to generate ideas for their topic (a mini-lesson that was taught 2 weeks earlier). Of these seven, five were able to make the progression from the web to a piece of writing that had a beginning, middle, and end.

Given the results of the data I have collected, it seems sensible to proceed in the following manner: First, I need to address the needs of the struggling readers and writers by breaking the writing process down into more manageable steps. I plan to do this in the form of mini-lessons at the beginning of each writing period for this small group. We will choose a topic, brainstorm or generate ideas, and create rough drafts together. Students will be taught to work with a peer for revising and editing.

Second, I have a large group of children who are spending the majority of their time in the drafting and illustrating stages. I plan to revisit prewriting strategies regularly for a few weeks until I see a greater number of students applying these strategies. I believe that I have moved too quickly in expecting these children to pick up on brainstorming and webbing. I will need to do a great deal more modeling for it to transfer to their writing. When I am satisfied that this is a tool that the students understand and are able to use, I will move on to creating a first draft or sloppy copy of the web and brainstorming sessions that I have created as examples. I think that spending more time on each phase will lead to more children reaching the revising and editing stages.

Final Thoughts

This research has provided me valuable information in assessing the productivity and value of the writer's workshop model as it exists in my classroom. While I found weak areas that need to be addressed, I also found children who greatly enjoy the freedom of choice. These children cannot wait to bring out their red folders and write about topics of utmost importance to them: broken arms, mothers with cancer, favorite pets, vacation trips, cherished holidays, and many others. One child recently reveled in the discovery that the red folder could be pulled out at any time during the day when he had a few extra minutes. The motivation to write exists. I now need to find the right combination of lessons to channel this desire through the stages of the writing process to publication.

SAMPLE 12.6
LINDA ROTH, ST. PETER SCHOOL DISTRICT, ST. PETER, MINNESOTA

This study was conducted by Linda Roth, a gifted education coordinator in St. Peter, Minnesota. She has included a short review of the literature at the beginning of her study. Notice how this serves to connect her observations with the ideas of others.

THE SOCIAL, EMOTIONAL, AND ACADEMIC ADJUSTMENT OF AN ACCELERATED ELEMENTARY STUDENT

This action research study investigated the social, emotional, and writing development of a student who moved directly from a fourth- to a sixth-grade classroom.

Background

Grade acceleration can have a positive effect on the achievement of gifted students (Davis & Rimm, 1998). This strategy allows students to advance at an appropriate pace in order to meet their education needs. Researchers studying acceleration find that there are very few problems with social adjustment, academic achievement, or other effects (Colangelo & Davis, 1991). Advantages included improved task commitment, confidence, and academic advances.

On average, gifted students who are accelerated do as well as or better than older students in the same classroom, their social and emotional development is normally quite high, and they are more inclined to choose older students as companions (Clark, 1983). Therefore, the issue of age and maturity does not seem to be of consequence here.

Those who are apprehensive about the practice of grade skipping are concerned that skill gaps may surface in basic areas. Barbara Clark (1983) recommends that accelerated students be monitored and continually assessed. When considering a student for acceleration it is important to have a thorough knowledge of the needs and abilities of that student with support from administration and staff at all stages (Gallagher & Gallagher, 1994).

Identification of the Action Research Problem

I work as a gifted and talented coordinator in the St. Peter, Minnesota, School District. A student in one of the elementary schools was accelerated from a fourth- to sixth-grade classroom. In this action research project I examined the social, emotional, and academic effects of this acceleration.

The Student

Bill was an 11-year-old male student. At the end of fourth grade he was going above and beyond the fourth-grade tasks assigned to him. His fourth-grade teacher described him as a good student, a nice person to talk to, and knowledgeable in many areas. He grasped concepts easily, finished assignments with time to spare, and completed extra assignments quickly. Other teachers who had worked with him gave him high praise for motivation, task commitment, and advanced knowledge. The hope was that by grade skipping, his enthusiasm would continue.

Behavior checklists completed by four teachers who had worked with him showed that he displayed many positive behaviors that might enable him to get along with his peers, function independently, and be successful academically.

On an academic achievement test Bill scored in the 95th percentile in reading and the 97th percentile in math. On a standardized ability test, he had an IQ score of 128, ranking him at the 97th percentile and classifying him in the superior range. On a standardized writing test it was found that his writing score was low because of the lack of sentence detail. Comments were made by the test facilitator and his fourth-grade teacher that while his sentence structure, legibility, spelling, capitalization, punctuation, and sentence structure were good, Bill did not go into a great deal of detail in his writing.

Implementation of the Action Research

This study was begun during the fall of Bill's sixth-grade year. The objective here was to find out how he was adjusting to skipping a grade, specifically in the area of writing. The social/emotional area was not a great concern to parents and teachers; however, for the well-being of Bill, I felt it important to also monitor this area of adjustment as it could have a bearing on the success of his acceleration.

Writing

Creative writing and expository writing samples were taken from Bill's sixth-grade classroom portfolio. Other writing samples were taken from short answer tests and email between Bill and me. These samples were evaluated using a writing rubric for middle school level performance. Format, mechanics, word choice, and organization were evaluated. In the creative writing samples, Bill's spelling, punctuation, and capitalization were of good quality. Words were used correctly and clearly; however, special or advanced vocabulary was not noted. In his expository writing, the introduction, paragraphs, and conclusions were present, but they were very brief and had little detail. No attempt was made to elaborate beyond that which was being asked.

After an email conversation with me and an interview with his classroom teacher regarding the importance of detail and elaboration, Bill was asked to write a creative story about a turkey. For this story, he was able to use his interest in technology and science. He wrote a four-page handwritten story about a turkey who lived in a space age city and visited a robot factory to obtain robot armor to protect himself from hunters of endangered species. This story ended with the explanation that it was all a dream sequence. This time more detail was evident, showing that Bill was capable of using detail and elaboration when writing about something that was of interest to him.

Social and Emotional Adjustment

Interviews with Bill were held weekly. In each of these he expressed great satisfaction with his new surroundings. Bill said that in sixth grade he was able to do whatever he wanted. He seemed to enjoy the freedom to make his own choices when assignments were completed. He also liked the responsibility of getting assignments done and turning them in on time.

Bill expressed concern about missing concepts in math; however, he felt that he generally got the ideas easily. His test results showed that he was not experiencing problems in this area. Bill also expressed concern about his art class. He felt he could put more effort into his drawings.

A goal Bill set at the beginning of the year was to get assignments in on time. He felt that he had met this goal. He also set a goal related to behavior, which was to not push people or interfere with their personal space. He felt this too had been met. Generally, Bill was pleased with his time management style and prided himself in completing his homework quickly.

Bill's sixth-grade teacher was interviewed regarding his social and emotional adjustment as well as his academic performance. His teacher was pleased with all areas of adjustment. Bill had made friends in the class and had found others with similar interests. He had made two close friendships and was spending time with one of them outside of school. This teacher said that Bill was highly respected for his intellect and was sought after by classmates for information and help in academic areas. Academically, Bill was doing well. The teacher reiterated that he grasped new concepts in math quickly and needed little repetition to master them.

Conclusions

Overall, grade acceleration seems to have been successful here. Positive social interactions and academic achievement have been noted. Extra attention to his writing needs to be continued during the remainder of the year. Support from the classroom teacher and me will be important to the success of this student. Monitoring the support of Bill should continue throughout the year to ensure that problem areas do not develop.

References

Clark, B. (1983). *Growing up gifted.* Columbus, OH: Merrill Publishing Company.

Colangelo, N., & Davis, G. (1991). *Handbook of gifted education.* Needham Heights, MA: Allyn and Bacon.

Davis, G. A., & Rimm, S. B. (1998). *Education of the gifted and talented* (4th ed.). Needham Heights, MA: Allyn and Bacon.

Gallagher, J. J., & Gallagher, S. A. (1994). *Teaching the gifted child* (4th ed.). Needham Heights, MA: Allyn and Bacon.

SAMPLE 12.7
ANGELA HASSETT BRUNELLE GETTY, MARTINEZ, CALIFORNIA

This study by Angela Hassett Brunelle Getty looks at gender and special education referrals. She does a nice job of connecting her findings to the research literature. Notice how she keeps things as simple as possible to create a report that is easy to read. Also, she uses tables to display her findings. This creates a very visual action research report that also enhances the readability. A simple, well-written report like this is much more apt to be read than one that is long and unorganized.

GENDER IMBALANCE IN SPECIAL EDUCATION
Purpose

This action research project was conducted to examine the relationship between gender and teacher referrals for special education services in our school. Do teachers possess certain biases toward males because of their behavior? Are males referred to Student Study Teams (SST) more often than females? How many of the students referred actually qualify for special education services?

Participants

Participants in this study were students from kindergarten through fifth grade in an elementary school with high state academic achievements. The student population at this school consisted of 66% White, 19% Asian,

6% Hispanic, 4% Other, 3% Black, and 2% Filipino. Instructional staff provided support to students through special programs such as reading specialist, counseling, special education, library, vocal and instrumental music, Gifted and Talented Education, physical education, and science and computer education.

Procedures

In our school, teachers refer students whom they suspect have special needs to a Student Study Team (SST). The SST then looks at various classroom data and that from psycho-educational assessment. This study examined the files of students who had been referred by their teacher to the Student Study Team (SST) during the 2002–2003 school year. There were 35 total files; 23 of them were active SST files and 12 had been resolved or were in process of a psycho-educational assessment. [Figure 12.5] shows the grade and gender breakdown.

After obtaining the permission of the vice principal, who is in charge of the SST process, student SST files and cumulative files were collected for those students whose teacher had initiated the SST process during some part of the 2002–2003 school year. Each student's file was then reviewed. Data were collected using a student data sheet. This was a data sheet designed to collect the following information: grade level, gender, month they were referred, reason for referral to the student study team, and if they qualified for special education services.

Files were reviewed to see if students were referred for behavior, academics, or both. In order to be consistent throughout the data collection

FIGURE 12.5   Files Examined for SST

GRADE	TOTAL	MALE	FEMALE
Kindergarten	3	1	2
1st	8	4	4
2nd	8	4	4
3rd	5	3	2
4th	9	5	4
5th	2	2	0
Total	35	19	16

process, <u>behavior</u> was the term used to indicate those instances where class-room teachers described a student using the terms "difficulty staying focused," "lacks motivation," "off task," "not independent," or "easily dis-tracted." <u>Academics</u> was the term used to indicate when a student was below grade level in specific academic areas.

Analysis

Data were analyzed by noting the referral totals and separating them by gender into the following three categories: behavior-only, academics-only, and behavior and academics. Also noted were the number of students referred to special education versus those who qualified for special educa-tion services. This too was broken down into gender categories.

Findings and Conclusions

Reasons for Referral

In our school, slightly more males than females were referred [see Fig-ure 12.6]. Slightly more males were referred for both behavior-only reasons as well as behavior and academics. Slightly more females were referred for academics-only.

Because of the limited numbers in this action research project, no strong conclusions can be made; however, the results seem to reflect the results of Phipps's (1982) study of 165 special education students. Phipps examined the differences between males and females in academic achieve-ment and behavior and looked at how this affected the referral process. In her study, behavior was the reason for referral in 83% of the cases for boys, but in only 45% of the cases for girls. She concluded that boys might be over-placed in special education classes to relieve the pressures of behavior management in the regular education classroom. Further, she posited that girls may be excluded from referral to special education programs because of their passive and more manageable behaviors. Lloyd, Kauffman, Landrum, &

FIGURE 12.6   Reasons for Referral to Student Study Teams

	TOTAL	MALE	FEMALE
Behavior-Only	11	7	4
Academics-Only	11	4	7
Behavior and Academics	13	8	5
Total Number of Students	35	19	16

Roe (1991) have also reported that boys outnumber girls in special education referrals by a ratio of more than 2:1. Higher referral rates have also been reported by Anderson (1997), Flynn and Rahbar (1994), MacMilliam, Gresham, Lopez, and Bocian (1996), McIntyre (1988), Shinn, Tindal, and Spira (1987), and Ysseldyke, Vanderwood, and Shriner (1997).

Qualifying for Special Education Services

This study found that of the students referred, there were slightly more females than males who actually qualified for the special education services [see Figure 12.7]. Of these, one female qualified was for academics-only and two females for behavior and academics. One male qualified for academics and behaviors. This may reflect the study by Flynn and Rahbar (1994) who found that girls seemed to be less likely to be referred and thus, under-identified for remedial services.

Plan of Action

Based on the information found in this study, I will be making the following suggestions to our school principal:

1. Teachers should be made aware of the general tendency to over-identify boys for referral to special education programs. I will recommend teacher inservices be conducted to inform teachers of this and provide instruction on behavior management techniques that would work specifically with the male population. Also, we may want to provide inservices on teaching practices that are less likely to cause behavior problems.

2. Because there are often fewer behavior problems, girls may be under-identified for referral. This is something that needs attention in the coming year. Again, teacher inservice and training should be made available to inform teachers of female learning styles.

FIGURE 12.7   Students Referred versus the Number Qualified for Special Education Services

	TOTAL	MALE	FEMALE
Number of Students Referred for Special Ed. Services	14	7	7
Number of Students Who Qualified for Special Ed. Services	4	1	3

3. Our school needs to have more prereferral interventions that are documented before students are referred for psycho-educational assessments. We should probably set up some procedures for this, with a variety of intervention strategies that could be used by classroom teachers.

4. We need to keep our eye on this issue. A study like this should be conducted every year.

References

Anderson, K. G. (1997). Gender bias and special education referrals. *Annals of Dyslexia, 47,* 151–162.

Flynn, J. M., & Rahbar, M. H. (1994). Prevalence of reading failure in boys compared with girls. *Psychology in Schools, 31,* 66–71.

Lloyd, J. W., Kauffman, J. M., Landrum, T. J., & Roe, D. L. (1991). Why do teachers refer pupils for Special Education? An analysis of referral records. *Exceptionality, 2,* 115–126.

MacMillian, D. L., Gresham, F. M., Lopez, M. F., & Bocian, K. (1996). Comparison of students nominated for prereferral interventions by ethnicity and gender. *The Journal of Special Education, 30,* 133–151.

McIntyre, L. (1988). Teacher gender: A predictor of special education referral? *Journal of Learning Disabilities, 21,* 382–383.

Phipps, P. A. (1982). The LD learner is often a boy—Why? *Academic Therapy, 17,* 425–430.

Shinn, M. R., Tindal, G. A., & Spira, D. A. (1987). Special Education referrals as an index of teacher tolerance: Are teachers imperfect tests? *Exceptional Children, 54,* 32–40.

Ysseldyke, J. E., Vanderwood, M. L., & Shriner, J. (1997). Changes over the past decade in special education referral to placement probability: An incredibly reliable practice. *Diagnostique, 23,* 193–201.

A FINAL WORD

The length and complexity of an action research project do not always increase its rigor and insight. Many short action research projects provide important insight and information. The goal of action research is to increase understanding in order to improve teaching practice. All the reports here meet this criterion.

WRITING AND REPORTING
ACTION RESEARCH

PRESENTING YOUR ACTION RESEARCH

If a teacher has a good idea in the middle of the forest but nobody is there to hear it, does that idea make a noise? This chapter talks about venues for sharing your action research.

THE EDUCATIONAL ENVIRONMENT

Your Colleagues

The most appreciative audience for presentations of your action research might be your colleagues. These presentations can take the form of a formal staff development inservice, a short talk at a regular faculty meeting, or simply a continued dialogue with colleagues. Whatever the form, these presentations promote conversation among teachers about the dynamics of their classrooms and various pedagogical methods and are essential for promoting reflection and growth in our profession.

When presenting action research projects, your findings are more apt to be attended to by your audience if you keep the presentation short and focused and include only those ideas that other teachers might use in their classroom. Presentations are also enhanced by including some kind of visual aid in the form of a poster, overhead, power point presentation, or handout. Always leave time for discussion at the end. Some aspects of a short presentation include the following:

1. *Your purpose.* Why did you choose to study what you did? Did a particular problem, special interest, or question lead you to your research? Describe your reasons for engaging in the action research project.
2. *Theoretical background.* Keep this short. If available, include some research or basic theoretical ideas related to your question, then link this to classroom practice.
3. *Data collection.* Describe the various forms of data and tell how you collected them.

4. *Findings.* Tell what you found. If your findings lend themselves to visual display, create a poster or handouts with the information in the form of a list, graph, or table.
5. *Conclusions.* What do your findings mean? What do they imply? What might be some of the reasons you came up with your findings? Again, keep this short.
6. *Your plan of action.* Tell what you plan to do or what you might do as a result of your findings. You might also ask teachers to brainstorm ideas for possible actions or possible solutions. This creates dialogue and allows teachers to share their ideas.
7. *Time for questions and discussion.* Finally, always leave time at the end of a presentation for questions and discussion.

Your Students

Your students will be interested to know what you found. After all, they have a vested interest in what goes on in your classroom. Also, action research mirrors the inquiry process, a powerful learning technique that you might consider using in your class. Inquiry is the process of designing learning activities that incorporate methods of science (Johnson, 2000). In doing inquiry, students are taught to ask a question and then to collect data to answer that question. In sharing your action research with your students you will be modeling the inquiry process as well as demonstrating methods for collecting and presenting data. Just as with teachers, allow and encourage questions and discussion. Students' thoughts and observations at the end of an action research study are often very apt and might even be included as a form of data in your final report.

School Boards, Principals, and Administrators: Making a Case

Decisions in education are sometimes made apart from a theoretical context or without considering any of the research related to learning and education. This can result in bad educational practice or educational malpractice. Action research can be used to enable your school or district to make informed decisions. It can also be used to make a case for employing a particular methodology or program. However, when doing action research to make a case, the onus is on you to keep an objective perspective during all phases of your research. That is, you must allow for the possibility that the literature or the data collected might disprove your original thesis.

Your Classroom: Evaluating New Programs

If you are piloting a new program, action research can be used as formative evaluation to see how things are going and what needs to be changed and as summative evaluation to judge the program's effectiveness. The key in using action research for evaluation is to keep the data collection simple and manageable. Do not let data collection get in the way of implementing the new program.

To illustrate how action research might be used in program evaluation, at Minnesota State University, Mankato, I piloted a new approach to my undergraduate literacy methods course. Students spent less time in my class listening to me speak (1 day a week) and more time in an elementary classroom practicing their teaching skills (3 days a week). Before I implemented the program, I made a plan to collect four types of data: (a) a pre- and poststudy survey of the undergraduate students, (b) a poststudy survey of teachers, (c) observations recorded using field notes, and (d) an analysis of students' reflections collected at eight points during the course of the semester. My goal was to see what was happening with this new approach, what was working, and what needed to be changed.

When the study was completed and the data compiled, I found that overall the new plan was fairly successful in helping to create knowledgeable, skillful teachers. My students could see how the ideas I presented in my methods classes applied to a classroom setting. But like any new program, it needed some tweaks and changes. The data collected was extremely useful in helping to pinpoint the changes that needed to be made. As a final step, I made a short presentation to the dean and to my colleagues at a faculty meeting. There I was able to make recommendations about future programs based on some solid data.

Parent Conferences

I remember as a beginning teacher feeling that I never had enough to say to parents at parent conferences. I was able to describe the child in terms of numbers using scores on standardized tests and homework assignments, but that was about it. As stated previously, many of the data collection methods described in Chapter 8 are forms of authentic assessment. The individual data related to each child can be used to provide a much clearer picture of who that child is as well as his or her strengths and interests.

Also, parents like to know what is happening in your classroom. Sharing your action research in a short newsletter gives them a sense of what is happening. It lets them know that your classroom is an intellectually vibrant place, and it shows that you are always looking for the best methods to use in helping their children grow and learn.

THE PROFESSIONAL ENVIRONMENT

Professional Conferences and Conventions

These days most researchers in education recognize the importance of including teachers' voices in the conversation. Professional conferences and teachers' conventions are a good place to create this conversation. I would recommend contacting local or state organizations that hold conventions and ask them to send you a proposal form. The proposal form you receive describes exactly what you need to include and usually needs to be returned 4 to 6 months before the conference date.

Academic Journals

You might consider sending your study to an academic journal. This is a good way to get your ideas out there for others to see and use. Start with state journals or smaller publications that are focused on areas related to your study. You can also get addresses and submission requirements for these as well as other important information at the following websites:

1. National Science Teachers Association Journals and Publications: www.nsta.org/journals
2. National Council for the Social Studies: www.socialstudies.org
3. International Reading Association: www.reading.org
4. National Council of Teachers of Mathematics: www.nctm.org
5. National Council of Teachers of English: www.ncte.org

Academic journals are peer reviewed, which means that two or more people look over your writing, make comments and suggestions (not always pleasant), and recommend whether to publish. Do not get discouraged, however, if you get your action research report back with a rejection or many suggestions for improvement. It is quite common for writers to have to revise several times before an article is finally accepted. Although this process may seem a little intimidating at first, getting feedback and specific comments is one of the best ways to improve your writing.

ERIC

ERIC stands for the Educational Resources Information Center. Sponsored by the National Library of Education at the U.S. Department of Education, it is a massive database containing information on all imaginable subjects related to education. ERIC collects documents such as curricula, articles, conference papers, essays, lesson plans, units, opinion papers, resource guides, technical reports, tests, questionnaires, measurement devices, books, research, and action research projects and makes them available to the educational community. You can send your documents to the following address:

ERIC Processing and Reference Facility
Acquisitions Department
4483-A Forbes Boulevard
Lanham, Maryland 20706

For more information, e-mail info@ericfac.piccard.csc.com, telephone 1-800-799-3742, or visit the website http://www.ericfacility.org/submitting.html.

LOCAL COMMUNITY ORGANIZATIONS

In most communities people outside education appreciate hearing about the latest teaching trends and ideas. Often, the perceptions these people have of education are based on their own experiences (which can be 20 to 40 years old), and what they read about in newspapers and magazines. Neither of these are very accurate sources. Presenting your action research at functions such as Rotary lunches, social and professional groups, religious organizations, parent organizations, or other types of gatherings provides people in your community with an updated version of the latest trends in education and, at the same time, generates good public relations for your school.

SUMMARY

- Your colleagues and students are often interested in hearing about the findings of your action research project.
- Action research can be used to make a case of a particular methodology or program or for evaluating new programs.
- The data collected in action research can be used to provide a more complete picture of your students.
- Professional conferences, academic journals, and the Education Resources Information Center are all viable venues for sharing your action research projects.
- Local community organizations are often interested in hearing of the latest trends in education and may also be a good place to present your action research findings.

WRITING AN ACTION RESEARCH REPORT

Unless you are making an oral presentation or conducting action research only for your own edification, you need to create some sort of written document describing your observation and findings. This chapter contains suggestions for writing an action research report.

An action research report is written using an academic writing style. Academic writing enhances the credibility of your report and increases the likelihood that it will be read. It is not within the scope of this book to describe at length the many parts of academic writing; however, a few tips concerning tone and style, length, and clarity are described in the following sections.

TONE AND STYLE

Academic writing is different from creative writing in that it is more concise and written as objectively as possible. The prime directive in academic writing is clear communication, thus, ideas are presented in a logical, orderly manner so that the reader is able to gain a maximum amount of understanding with a minimum amount of time and effort.

Traditional, experimental research is written in a very objective style. You will not find any "I," "you," or "me" pronouns; only the facts described in third person. Personal observations are saved for a special section at the end of the report and are also written in third person. The goal in experimental research reports is to eliminate any bias or subjectivity on the part of the researcher and allow only the data to speak.

Action research, however, is written in a more subjective style. It is recognized that you are part of the research; thus, your thoughts and observations are valued and are recorded along the way. (You can see this personal, reflective writing style in the sample research reports in Chapter 12.) But keep in mind that an action research report is not a letter to the editor. Pronounced biases or hidden agendas are fairly easy to spot and detract from your accuracy and credibility.

In your action research report, you must demonstrate that your descriptions are fair and honest if your research is to be given credence. Consider the following examples:

LESS EFFECTIVE

I really believe that schools should throw away those disgusting state standards that require that certain things be taught in a certain way. These outrageous mandates are an insult to our hard-working, knowledgeable teachers who know best how to meet the needs of students. It also sucks all the joy and creativity out of teaching.

MORE EFFECTIVE

Teachers can become more effective when they have a certain amount of freedom in determining what is taught, and when they are able to design learning experiences in a way that best matches our teaching style and the needs of our students. State mandates do not always allow us to make the best choices or to utilize our creativity.

Avoid using value statements, highly charged language, and emotional buzzwords:

LESS EFFECTIVE

In my opinion, using invented spelling is the best strategy I have ever seen for helping young children learn to write. I really like the way that students in this study thought about the message instead of worrying about correct spelling. And don't forget all the excitement that was generated as students eagerly shared their wonderful new creations with each other. And of course, there was the pride of taking home a finished product to share with parents. Using invented spelling helped to produce elaborate and imaginative ideas, helped children organize their writing, and created an environment that is very productive and enjoyable. Invented spelling is a must for primary students.

MORE EFFECTIVE

Invented spelling seems to have been effective in helping young children learn to write. Children in my classroom were able to concentrate on communicating their ideas rather than worrying about spelling. They seemed to create writing that was more elaborate and better organized than when they were using conventional spelling. They also seemed to enjoy sharing their ideas in these settings. It seems that invented spelling is an effective technique to use in moving children toward mature writing.

LENGTH

How long should your action report be? Long enough to say it; short enough so as not to bore or confuse the reader. This means using as few words as possible. There is nothing more frustrating than having to sort through a thick forest of words to try to find an author's point. If you use too many words, your ideas are obscured and you lose the reader. Using fewer words increases the likelihood of your report being read and understood. In your action research reports, always consider what does not need to be there. Good writers know how to state their ideas using a minimum number of words.

LESS EFFECTIVE

I believe that writing is extremely important because it helps my students organize their thinking. This is helpful. All people, students as well as adults, should try to develop their writing skills. This will help in their school lives as well as in their careers. Writing forces you to think through your ideas before you begin writing. You have to record your ideas to see what it is you believe about a thing. Also, the very act of generating ideas helps you to see the relationships between more things. This is what creativity is. Creativity has to do with seeing connections, associations, and relationships. Thinking also shapes our writing. Sometimes you do not know exactly what it is you are going to say. When you write, you see your thoughts hung out in space, frozen in time. The advantage of writing is that you can go back and tweak it to get it just right before you deliver the message.

MORE EFFECTIVE

Writing shapes thinking by helping the writer to generate ideas, see relationships, and put ideas in an organized form. However, thinking also shapes writing. With writing, we can see our thoughts, organize them, and edit them to get them just right before we deliver them.

CLARITY

The clarity of your final report should be such that another person could read it and duplicate your steps. As stated above, clarity can be enhanced by using as few words as possible. It can also be enhanced by entering a teaching mode; that is, you assume that the reader knows nothing and you must explain to them what you did and what you saw.

Clarity can also be enhanced by the organization of your report. To organize your thoughts, first create an outline so that you are able to see the logical structure of your report. Then, use headings and subheadings to let the reader see the structure and to show when you move from one major idea to the next.

HEADINGS

Below is an example of a short section I wrote that enters into a teaching mode but does not use headings.

Consciousness

Consciousness is that which we choose to be aware of, both internally and externally. Consciousness is a composite of those thoughts and images that we attend to. Jungian theory describes four levels of consciousness.

Collective consciousness is the outer world of values and perceptions that a society shares. Here every stimulus has a response. Machines have gears, springs, and levers, all operating according to the laws of physics. All physical effects spring from physical causes, and time is conceived of in strictly linear terms. This is the objective outer world where reality is determined by repeatability and the laws of cause and effect.

The collective unconscious is a part of the human psyche that is shared by all. An illustrative metaphor might be to think of it as psychic cyberspace to which every human is connected. Here, every thought, action, and emotion ever experienced by humanity is embedded and available to us in the form of archetypal images. Archetypal images are those images formed around patterns within the collective unconscious and birthed into human consciousness as symbols and motifs.

Personal consciousness or ego is the thinking with which we are consciously aware. This can include logical reasoning as well as emotions and intuition. To expand personal consciousness, one becomes aware of a wider variety of stimuli, both internal and external. This can be done through meditation or simply slowing the mind and concentrating on being aware.

The personal unconscious is the layer of thinking not readily accessible to our conscious mind. Contained here is material that has reached consciousness and been forgotten, such as repressed memories, emotions, and personal experiences. It also contains material that has not yet reached consciousness, such as archetypal images. This is the subjective inner world where reality is determined by meaning. That is, the images perceived here are real in so far as they have some meaning or significance for us.

Now here is the same piece of writing with the headings inserted. Notice the difference in the clarity and understanding.

Consciousness

Consciousness is that which we choose to be aware of, both internally and externally. Consciousness is a composite of those thoughts and images that we attend to. Jungian theory describes four levels of consciousness.

Collective Consciousness

Collective consciousness is the outer world of values and perceptions that a society shares. Here every stimulus has a response. Machines have gears, springs, and levers, all operating according to the laws of physics. All physical effects spring from physical causes, and time is conceived of in strictly linear terms. This is the objective outer world where reality is determined by repeatability and the laws of cause and effect.

The Collective Unconscious

The collective unconscious is a part of the human psyche that is shared by all. An illustrative metaphor might be to think of it as psychic cyberspace to which every human is connected. Here, every thought, action, and emotion ever experienced by humanity is embedded and available to us in the form of archetypal images. Archetypal images are those images formed around patterns within the collective unconscious and birthed into human consciousness as symbols and motifs.

Personal Consciousness

Personal consciousness or ego is the thinking with which we are consciously aware. This can include logical reasoning as well as emotions and intuition. To expand personal consciousness, one becomes aware of a wider variety of stimuli, both internal and external. This can be done through meditation or simply slowing the mind and concentrating on being aware.

Personal Unconscious

The personal unconscious is the layer of thinking not readily accessible to our conscious mind. Contained here is material that has reached consciousness and been forgotten, such as repressed memories, emotions, and personal experiences. It also contains material that has not yet reached consciousness, such as archetypal images. This is the subjective inner world where reality is determined by meaning. That is, the images perceived here are real in so far as they have some meaning or significance for us.

For specific information related to both the process of academic writing and the form that product should take, I would direct you to *A Short Guide to Academic Writing* (Johnson, 2003a). This text will teach you the basics of academic writing using APA 5th edition style manual (American Psychological Association, 2001).

SUMMARY

- Using an academic style of writing in your action research report enhances its credibility and makes it more likely to be read.
- Academic writing is an objective style of writing in which as few words as possible are used in describing data and ideas.
- The clarity of your action research report is enhanced by entering a teaching mode and by using headings and subheadings.

QUESTIONS AND ACTIVITIES

1. Select a letter to the editor from a newspaper. First, list the facts presented, then report the author's ideas using a purely subjective tone.
2. Find a paragraph in a textbook, newspaper, or magazine. Lengthen it by adding words to it while retaining the original meaning. Then, trade your paragraph with a partner and take out all the words that do not need to be there.
3. Go on a treasure hunt. Find the following: (a) a concise, well-written paragraph, (b) a confusing paragraph, (c) a paragraph with a lot of extra words and sentences, and (d) a paragraph that seems overly biased or subjective.

ACTION RESEARCH AS MASTER'S THESIS

I would encourage those of you who are in graduate programs in education to consider doing an action research project for your master's thesis. In advising graduate students over the years, I have found that writers tend to find these projects more interesting and enjoyable to do. Action research projects are also more apt to affect their classroom practice. Not coincidentally, these projects usually seem to be more interesting to read and of better quality.

BEFORE YOU START

The graduate thesis represents the culminating experience of a graduate program. In it you must demonstrate that you are able to utilize academic sources to come to a conclusion in a way that will move the field forward. Below are nine tips and a flexible guide to use in structuring your action research thesis. Note, however, that colleges and universities have varying requirements for the master's thesis.

Nine Tips for Writing Your Master's Thesis

1. *See your advisor before beginning your graduate paper.* It is recommended that the first consultation occur at least one year and not less than 6 months before the projected completion. It takes a great deal of time to comprehend and synthesize all the ideas necessary for a graduate thesis. Your goal is to create a professional paper that contributes to the field, and this cannot be done in a few weeks.

2. *Decide on a topic or area of research first, then put it in the form of a question or questions.* A clear focus saves you much time in your research and results in a tighter and more coherent paper.

3. *Keep your thesis proposal short and flexible.* Most graduate programs ask students to write a thesis proposal. This is a very short description of your research project with 5 to 10 literature sources used to put your research question into a theoretical context. Proposals usually have to be preapproved by a graduate committee and the department of graduate studies at your school before you begin. Your initial proposal is a flexible guideline of your intended research project. It is very common for the final product to look somewhat different from the proposal.

4. *Do not expect your advisor to be an editor.* The onus is ultimately on you to write in a logical, coherent, objective style that can be easily understood by all who read your paper. An advising professor will provide feedback and some editorial comments, but this is much different from taking on the role of an editor.

5. *Start collecting journal articles for your literature review as soon as possible.* All master's papers contain a review of the literature related to the topic or research question. A number of sources are needed. (I tell my graduate students that a minimum of 25 is needed.) These sources must be from current texts or juried academic journals (see your advisor if you have questions here). It takes time to read, take notes, and synthesize all the material you read; thus, allow plenty of time for this stage. Some graduate students try to take shortcuts at this stage; however, I have found that these shortcuts always end up being "long cuts."

6. *Create a preliminary outline for your literature review.* An outline is used to help you find a logical structure. This structure is like the frame of a house and is used to hold your ideas together. Some like to use an inverted triangle that goes from most general to most specific. For example, if I were writing a paper on gifted learners and reading in the elementary school, I would use the following sections: (a) gifted learners, (b) reading in the elementary school, and (c) gifted learners and reading in the elementary school.

7. *Begin to plan how you will collect data.* Teachers often use a pilot study in their class to experiment with and refine several data collection methods before selecting those they will use. Keep in mind that your data collection must be well planned and systematic.

8. *Plan on revising each chapter at least four times.* Revision is what separates good writing from average writing. Revision is at the heart of writing of any kind.

9. *Assume the reader knows nothing.* Adopt a teaching, describing mode. The reader should know exactly what you are doing and why, and be able to replicate your procedures.

THE ACTION RESEARCH THESIS

Described next are the parts that might make up a master's thesis using action research. This is not meant to be a recipe; rather, it is a very flexible guideline. The order and parts to be included may vary depending on your research topic and the requirements of your college or university. Your advisor may also ask for slight variations of this form; thus, it is imperative that you meet with your advisor *before* you begin! This will save you both a great deal of time and help you avoid frustration.

CHAPTER I
INTRODUCTION

1. Introduction to the Topic (no heading for this section)
    A. Identify the problem or area of interest.
    B. Provide background information.
2. Purpose Statement (heading, centered)
    A. State purpose of paper/study. Example: *The purpose of this paper was to examine the writing workshop in my second grade and to describe effective implementation practices.*
    B. Put the purpose in the form of one or more questions. Example: *The specific research questions are:*
        1. *What is happening during my writing workshop?*
        2. *Is the writing workshop effective in developing my students' writing skills?*
        3. *If so, how should the writing workshop be implemented in a primary grade setting?*
3. Importance of the Study (heading, centered)
    A. Tell why this study is important.
    B. Example: *The information here will be of value to . . . It will also provide elementary teachers with a plan to . . .*
4. Definition of Terms (heading, centered)
    A. List important terms.
    B. Briefly describe each term using one or two complete sentences.

CHAPTER II
REVIEW OF THE LITERATURE

1. This builds the foundation for your thesis. Here you provide background information to support your question or to put your research topic in a theoretical context. Also, you want to see what others have found related to your topic that may be of use in your action research.
2. Gather material. Consider using 25–40 sources. Use current, peer-reviewed journal articles whenever possible.
3. After reading each piece, take notes listing the citation at the top and only those items of importance below. Use headings whenever possible. This will make it easier to organize your notes.
4. Begin thinking about the structure. Some people like to web or outline to find structure initially. As data in the form of your notes are gathered,

begin to look for categories. Your initial structures should be very flexible because they most likely will change.

5. As you write this chapter, use headings and subheadings to break up the text. It is very hard to read several pages of text without headings.

6. Describe empirical research related to your topic. When describing research studies, try to use one or two sentences to describe each of the following: (a) the question or purpose of the study, (b) the number and type of participants, (c) the treatment or conditions involved, (d) the type of measures, and (e) the results and conclusions.

7. This chapter ends with a brief summary of the major points covered that is generally about one paragraph in length. Sometimes the summary is put in list form with each point cited.

CHAPTER III
METHODOLOGY

1. Participants (heading, centered)
   A. Describe the people involved. The reader should know ages, number, gender, ethnic makeup, and anything else you feel is pertinent to your research.
   B. Describe the environment: classroom, school, or community.
2. Materials (heading, centered)
   A. Describe any materials used in your research. If you are using a particular curriculum, product, or procedure, describe it fully. Include relevant examples in an appendix. Remember that the reader knows nothing.
   B. Describe all types of measuring devices. If surveys, checklists, rubrics, or rating charts are used, describe them briefly, then include a sample in the appendix.
3. Procedures (heading, centered)
   A. Describe the length of the study.
   B. Describe how you collected the data, how much, and how often.
   C. Use past tense in describing all aspects of your methodology and findings. Research always exists in the past, in a specific time and place.
   D. If you use a special curriculum, technique, or procedure, let the reader know exactly what it is. This section should be described in such a way that one could pick up this chapter and replicate your procedures.

4. Analysis (heading, centered)
  A. Describe how you will organize and analyze your data. Inductive analysis will most likely be used for your field notes and other qualitative data.
  B. Quantitative data will generally be analyzed using totals and mean scores. Here a simple comparative analysis will be made. It is outside the scope of this book to talk about statistical methods; however, statistical analysis is also an option.

CHAPTER IV
FINDINGS

1. Restate your research questions.
2. Describe the data that answer that question (this chapter is often the longest chapter in an action research thesis).
3. Describe the themes, categories, and patterns.
4. Use illustrative examples for each category.
5. Use tables, graphs, figures, and artwork as necessary.
6. Use headings and subheadings to make the structure readily apparent.

CHAPTER V
DISCUSSION

1. Overview of the Study (heading, centered)
  A. Restate the general purpose of the study.
  B. Briefly describe how the results were obtained.
2. Summary of Findings (heading, centered)
  A. Provide a brief summary of the findings.
  B. This may be one to two paragraphs.
3. Conclusions (heading, centered)
  A. Move beyond the data. Tell what these results mean.
  B. Describe possible implications of the results.
4. Recommendations (heading, centered)
  A. Describe how the results might be used in your classroom.
  B. Describe how the results may be used to bring understanding to other classrooms or situations.
  C. Sometimes the conclusions and recommendations merge.
5. Limitations of the Study (heading, centered)
  A. Describe those things that may have hindered or affected your findings.

B. Describe those things that you needed to change during the study, or things that did not go as expected. Remember, a good study is not one that proves your particular point; rather, a good study is one that looks carefully, reports accurately, and fairly represents the bit of reality that you experienced.

C. Describe the limitations or applicability of the findings. For example, your recommendations might be applied only to a certain segment of the population. Also, were you able to look at all facets of the problem?

D. Describe ideas for future research related to your research.

THE LAST WORD

I have found that graduate students like to have some idea of what goes into a thesis; however, I once again reiterate: The structure described above is a *flexible guideline* that should be adapted to meet the needs of your particular research question.

THE LITERATURE REVIEW

A THEORETICAL CONTEXT

As described previously, a literature review is used to set your ideas in a theoretical context. You synthesize what the literature says about your research topic, then report it in an organized fashion. Chapter 7 identified the possible sources for the literature review as: academic journals, the Internet, books, and nonprint sources. Again, the number of sources used is dictated solely by your question and the purpose of your study.

Steps for a Literature Review

It is common to spend a great deal of time during the beginning stages of an action research project simply reading articles and taking notes. Although this may seem time consuming initially, it makes the research and writing process more efficient and effective. Steps to use in gathering data for your literature review follow:

Step 1: Find a Good College Library

Public libraries usually do not have the academic journals and books needed to complete a literature review. Most college libraries do have a wide variety of academic journals as well as recent books published in the area of education.

Step 2: Locate Possible Sources

The library you use will have some type of computer database system in which all its journal articles and books are entered by subject, author, and key words. When you enter your topic in the search engine, the database provides you with one or more entries that look something like this:

> Johnson, A. (1998). What exactly are comprehension skills and how do I teach them? *Reading, 32*(2), 22–26.

This entry tells you the author (Johnson, A.), the year the article was published (1998), the title of the article ("What Exactly Are Comprehension Skills and How

Do I Teach Them?"), the name of the journal (*Reading*), the volume (32), the journal number within that volume (2), and the page numbers on which it can be found (pages 22–26).

Most libraries organize their journals and magazines alphabetically by journal title. Once you locate the journal, the year and volume number should be listed on the front cover. When journals are 2 years old or older, libraries usually take all the journals from a particular year or volume and bind them up in book form. This makes the journals easier to find and helps them last longer.

For example, to find the article above, go to the R section of the journals and magazines until you find the journal, *Reading.* Then look for volume number 32 (several *Reading* journals will be listed as volume 32), and find the second journal (number 2) published within that volume. The article will be found on page 22 of that journal.

Sometimes, journals are organized by Library of Congress number. On the computer screen the number will look something like this:

LB 1101. R2

Go to the journals found in the L section (these will all be journals of similar topics). Then move down until you find the LB section, then the 1101s, and, finally, 1101.R2.

In another database all the books contained at that library are categorized and described. To locate relevant books, enter the title, author, or subject. Books may be organized either by Library of Congress numbers or the Dewey Decimal number. In all cases, if you are lost or confused (a very common experience), find a librarian. They are usually glad to help. I recommend using journal articles instead of books for the majority of your sources because they are more current, more focused, and they allow you to get a great amount of information from a variety of sources in a short amount of time.

Step 3: Peruse Your Sources

After you get a pile of books or journals, find a table and take a few minutes to see whether your sources provide information related to your question. For books, look at the table of contents and the index and skim a few chapters. For journal articles, read the abstract and scan the headings, subheadings, and final paragraph. A few minutes here saves you much time later on. It also prevents you from having to carry around a pile of books and journals.

Step 4: Take Careful Notes

When taking notes, first record the full reference citation at the top of the page. Having the citation here saves you the task of looking up the articles again when creating the reference page. Next, record your notes using only one side of the page. This allows you to spread all your notes out in front of you when you begin to write your first draft.

To illustrate this process, I have included some of the notes that I used in writing an article about using literacy techniques to attend to the emotional needs of gifted students (Johnson, 2003b). In taking notes, I recorded only the information that was needed to support the question: How can we use literacy to attend to the emotions needs of gifted students? These notes were written using short sentences that were often incomplete. The goal during note-taking is not to create grammatically correct writing; rather, it is to restate and remember the author's ideas in a way that makes them readily accessible to you.

NOTES FOR ARTICLE

Shaker, P. (1982). The application of Jung's analytical psychology to education. *Journal of Curriculum Studies, 14,* **241–250.**

1. Jung was empiricist, studying the subjective psyche objectively.
   A. Used objective to study the subjective.
2. Political structure of academia has lead to neglect of Jung's work.
3. Process of development = individuation or self-realization.
   A. Birth and transformation of ego.
4. Myth provides a means for analyzing issues of existence.
5. Process of development: individuation or self-realization.
   A. Transformation of ego.
6. Educators can employ elements of analytic psychology.
   A. Attend to concepts of multiple realities.
   B. Look at symbols within literature.

Lovecky, D. V. (1998). Spiritual sensitivity in gifted children. *The Roeper Review, 20,* **178–183.**

1. Many gifted children appear to explore spiritual concepts.
2. Take delight in exploring spiritual questions.

Russel-Chapin, L. A., Rybak, C. J., & Copilevitz, T. B. (1996). The art of teaching Jungian analysis. *Journal of Humanistic Education and Development, 34,* **171–181.**

1. For Jung, life is a process of becoming more fully and wholly one's self (self-realization).
   A. Opposing parts of personality become more integrated.
2. Need to recognize and address the influence of the unconscious.
3. Ego = part of person which they permit themselves to be consciously aware of.
   A. The process of individuation, ego shifts inward.
   B. Towards subjective perspective.

Smith, C. D. (1990). Religion and crisis in Jungian analysis. *Counseling and Values, 34,* 177–186.

1. Underling cause of meaninglessness is in psychic fragmentation.
   A. Arises when individual is cut off from unconscious content.
   B. Cure is also found in unconscious.
2. Analytical process = establishing contact with unconscious.
   A. Dream analysis, active imagination, artistic experiences.

Step 5: Create a Rough Draft and Start the Revision Process

The next step is to look for groups of ideas and begin writing a rough first draft. This is followed by a series of revisions in which you revisit your notes and continue refining your document.

Using an Objective Writing Style

Your literature review is much more convincing when you use objective language and let the ideas speak for themselves. This means avoiding value statements and highly charged language in your writing.

Avoiding Value Statements.   A value statement states what you believe without offering support. You can avoid these by creating sentences that state an idea and then support it.

LESS EFFECTIVE

Teachers really need to learn how to differentiate the curriculum so that they can meet the needs of highly able and less able learners.

MORE EFFECTIVE

Learning how to differentiate the curriculum will help teachers meet the needs of both highly able and less able learners.

LESS EFFECTIVE

A study by Jones (2002) reveals a startling statistic: low ability readers spend the majority of their reading class engaged in mindless skills instruction apart from any meaningful context and do very little reading for pleasure. Is it any wonder that these students hate to read?

MORE EFFECTIVE

A study by Jones (2002) showed that low ability readers spend the majority of reading class time engaged in isolated skills instruction with very little time spent on pleasurable reading. Doing more free reading for pleasure in reading class may increase the amount of voluntary reading done outside of class.

You can avoid creating value statements also by not using value words such as *must, should,* and *needs to be.* Instead, say it and support it.

LESS EFFECTIVE

It is important for educators to use real literature in their reading courses. They should also utilize an aesthetic response whenever possible.

MORE EFFECTIVE

Using real literature in reading courses enhances a reading program. This type of material more closely reflects authentic reading experiences and allows for an element of choice by both teachers and students. And, instead of utilizing an efferent response to literature where students are asked to recount story details, requiring an aesthetic response allows students to respond with their ideas and emotions. This too, is a closer approximation of authentic reading experiences.

LESS EFFECTIVE

Educators need to recognize other forms of intelligence.

MORE EFFECTIVE

Recognizing other forms of intelligence will help educators develop the full potential of all their students.

A SAMPLE LITERATURE REVIEW

Below is a sample of part of an article written to describe how elementary teachers might incorporate classroom computers into their reading curriculums when they only have one or two in their classrooms. I used eight sources here to set my ideas in a theoretical context.

INTEGRATING CLASSROOM COMPUTERS
INTO A READING CURRICULUM

Most elementary classrooms today also have one or two computers; however, these computers are often used only for administrative purposes or for playing games, instead of being used for learning (McCannon & Crews,

2000). Teachers sometimes feel they do not have the time, resources, or knowledge necessary to effectively integrate computers into teaching and learning (Hoffman, 1997; Smith-Gratto & Fisher, 1999). This article describes some several very simple ideas and activities that can be used to integrate two classroom computers into a reading curriculum.

Computer-Integrated Learning in the Classroom

This article describes how one or two classroom computers can be integrated into a reading curriculum. There are four benefits of integrating computers into a classroom curriculum:

1. *Computer-based learning allows students' individual learning needs to be met* (Bagui, 1998; Chisholm & Wetzel, 1997; Ertmer, Addison, Lane, Ross, & Woods, 1999). With computer-based learning, students can work at their own rate in a nonthreatening environment. This frees up the teacher to spend more time with students who need extra help. Also, students can work to improve specific content area skills and knowledge.

2. *Computers enhance students' writing skills* (Chisholm & Wetzel, 1997). Writing on the computer does not seem to be as permanent as writing on paper; therefore, students are more willing to take risks and write more creatively. Editing and revising are easier to do on the computer than on handwritten stories. It is much easier to move things around and change the order of your words, sentences, and paragraphs. Students who have difficulties with handwriting due to fine motor skills can overcome them by writing with a keyboard.

3. *Computers create opportunities for students to do meaningful work and make connections with things outside of school* (Peck & Dorricott, 1994). Students can create products that have value outside of the school such as web pages, presentations, brochures, and flyers for a multitude of purposes. They might also write stories and poems and submit them for publication or post them on the Internet and receive feedback.

4. *Students have access to a wide variety of up-to-date information through the Internet and CD-ROMs.* Access to the World Wide Web provides students with unlimited information on almost any subject instantly. Information here can be used to enhance or provide background information on stories, books, or various class topics. Also, e-mail correspondence allows students to have direct contact with people, schools, and businesses around the world.

Computer Labs

Most schools have some sort of computer lab; however, this is not always the most effective method for integrating computers into classroom instruction for two reasons. First, instruction in the computer lab may not be related to learning that is happening in the regular classroom. Instruction here is often taught by a specialist teacher and as a result, the activities done during this period are often isolated computer skills lessons that do not integrate ideas and skills from the classroom (Ely, 1993).

Second, computer labs provide limited access to computers. Because computer labs are shared by many classrooms, fairly rigid schedules must be prepared in advance. This creates restricted opportunities for teachers to use the computer lab. Also, the hassles involved in scheduling a computer lab and marching students down to a separate facility often prevents teachers from integrating computers into their daily lessons. As a result, students may have access to computers only once or twice a week for 30 to 50 minutes. In this situation, computers have minimal impact on learning.

THE REFERENCE PAGE

Any article or book that is referred to in your text must appear on the reference page at the end of that text. This informs readers as to what sources were used and allows them to locate these sources if necessary. Below is the reference page for the article above.

REFERENCES

Bagui, S. (1998). Reasons for increased learning using multimedia. *Journal of Educational Multimedia and Hypermedia, 7*(1), 3–18.

Chisholm, I. M., & Wetzel, K. (1997). Lessons learned from a technology-integrated curriculum for multi-cultural classrooms. *Journal of Technology and Teacher Education, 5*(4), 293–317.

Ely, D. (1993). Computers in schools and universities in the United States of America. *Educational Technology, 33*(9), 53–57.

Ertmer, P. A., Addison, P., Lane, M., Ross, E., & Woods, D. (1999). Examining teachers' beliefs about the role of technology in the elementary classroom. *Journal of Research on Computing, 32*(1), 54–72.

Hoffman, B. (1997). Integrating technology into schools. *The Education Digest, 62*(5), 51–55.

McCannon, M., & Crews, T. B. (2000). Assessing the technology training needs of elementary school teachers. *Journal of Technology and Teacher Education, 8*(2), 111–121.

Peck, K., & Dorricott, D. (1994). Why use technology? *Educational Leadership, 51*(4), 11–14.

Smith-Gratto, K., & Fisher, M. (1999). An aid to curriculum and computer integration: Prototypes for teachers. *Computers in the Schools, 15*(2), 61–71.

SUMMARY

- A literature review sets your ideas in a theoretical context.
- The number of sources used for a literature review varies depending on the question and the purpose of your study.
- Possible sources to use for a review of the literature include academic journals, the Internet, books, and nonprint sources.
- The steps in creating a literature review are to (a) find a good college library, (b) locate possible sources, (c) peruse your sources, (d) take careful notes, and (e) begin the draft and revision process.
- Using an objective writing style that avoids value statements creates a more convincing document.
- Any book or article that you cite in your text must be listed on your reference page at the end of your report.

QUESTIONS AND ACTIVITIES

1. Find an example of an article in an academic journal that has a well-written literature review. What traits or attributes lead you to believe this review is well written?
2. Identify a topic that interests you. Find two articles related to this topic. Synthesize the information and report it in an organized fashion using no more than two double-spaced pages.
3. What is an effective practice or program that you support or that you believe should be instituted in your classroom or in schools. Find an article in an academic journal that supports your view and write one to two paragraphs to make your case using objective, academic language.
4. Find in a newspaper a letter to the editor with which you agree. Take out all the value statements and list just the facts. Make a case to support the position using objective, academic language.
5. Find in a newspaper a letter to the editor with which you disagree. Take out all the value statements and list just the facts. Make a case to support the position using objective, academic language.

FINDINGS: REPORTING QUALITATIVE DATA

Presenting the data you collected in your action research project may comprise the bulk of your report. You use your data to create a picture that describes what you found. The goal is to transform your field notes and other data into a form that can be easily digested (Taylor & Bogdan, 1998). Do not try to recount and report every bit of data collected because you will overwhelm and bore your reader. Instead, describe the meaningful trends, patterns, and categories you found and include representative samples so that the reader gets a sense of what you discovered. In this sense you are representing a particular view of reality (yours).

PRESENTING QUALITATIVE DATA

You can be creative in how you present the data as long as you describe your experiences fairly and adequately. Five tips can help you create an effective writing tone and style.

1. *Try to be an impartial reporter.* Action researchers realize that it is impossible to be totally impartial; however, you should fairly represent all aspects of what you are studying. In your writing tone, avoid letter-to-the-editor syndrome. As described previously, you create a more credible document when you simply state and support your ideas and avoid using value statements.

LESS EFFECTIVE

The observations in this study clearly demonstrate the absurdity of those misinformed educators who insist that time spent reading good books in reading class is wasted time.

MORE EFFECTIVE

The observations showed that allowing time for voluntary reading in reading class has some very positive effects.

2. *Include yourself when it is warranted.* It is acceptable to use the *I* pronoun when describing something that you did or observed (McNiff et al., 1996). You are, after all, a part of the study; thus, you should refer to yourself in a personal way instead of using an impersonal form, such as, *the researcher.*

LESS EFFECTIVE

For this study, the researcher spent 7 weeks observing students in a second-grade classroom.

MORE EFFECTIVE

For this study, I spent 7 weeks observing students in my second-grade classroom.

3. *Take readers along with you in all phases of your study.* Let them inside your head so they know exactly what you did and why you did it. To do this, your action research report should describe some or all of the following: (a) your question or focus, (b) the present environment or conditions, (c) what data you plan to collect, (d) the methods used to collect the data, (e) the data, (f) your thoughts along the way, and (g) how the data might be applied or used to understand other situations. The rule of thumb is that a reader should be able to replicate your procedure.

Teresa Van Batavia wrote in such a way that we knew *exactly* what she was doing (her complete project is included in Chapter 12):

WRITING WORKSHOP

My first-grade students at Eisenhower Elementary are involved in a writer's workshop setting at least three times a week. My concern is that children may be slipping through the cracks—doing little or no writing and not being noticed.

Data Collection

The first form of data collection that I used is that of a weekly checklist. As I circulated among students during the 2-week period from November 15 through December 3, 1999, I carried a clipboard and checked off each type of writing activity that I observed [see Figure 12.4]. This checklist became an effective tool for helping me to choose mini-lesson topics for the children. I will continue to use this on an informal basis throughout the year.

In addition to the checklists, I met individually with each student and also collected their writing folders for further study of their writing habits. Following are my notes of these conferences.

4. *Write clearly and precisely.* As stated previously, too many words are just as damaging to comprehension as too few words. Be selective in what you choose to report. The goal is to get maximum communication using a minimum of words. A clear, concise paper is more apt to be read. A long, rambling paper is more apt to be ignored.

5. *Organize your paper.* You have a certain amount of freedom in the structure or form of your research report. That is, you are not bound by the same confines that dictate empirical research studies; however, the onus is on you to create a paper that can be easily understood. One way to do this is to organize your paper so that the structure is readily apparent to the reader. The next section describes this.

THE IMPORTANCE OF STRUCTURE

Structure is the essence of all things. In writing, structure is the skeleton used to carry your ideas.

Structure and Inductive Analysis

One way to create structure for your paper is to use the process of inductive analysis described in Chapter 9:

1. Gather data and collect notes.
2. Spread out your notes in front of you.
3. Look for common ideas.
4. Move common ideas into groups to create sections.
5. Within each section, look for similar items to create paragraphs or subsections.

Using Headings to Create Structure

Using heads makes a report easier to read. Below is a writing sample that does not use headings. To the reader it appears as a large blob of text. Large blobs like this are less reader friendly because the structure is indistinct.

MS. BAKER'S WRITING WORKSHOP

In November 1996, I spent 2 weeks in Ms. Baker's second-grade classroom watching her writing workshop. Here writing was taught as a process consisting of five stages: prewriting, first draft, revising, editing, and publication. Student choice was integral to this process. Ms. Baker said that allowing students to choose their own writing topics seemed to result in a better quality of writing. Students' writing often reflected events going on in their lives, thus increasing feelings of ownership and emotional attachment. They seemed eager to share their ideas and experiences using writing.

Conversation was an integral part of the writing workshop. Students talked about possible writing topics, about their current writing projects, and about things happening in their lives. More formal conversations related directly to students' writing occurred in individual and small-group conferences and in large-group sharing sessions.

Skills identified in language arts manuals and unit tests were taught using explicit instruction in short minilessons lasting 5 to 10 minutes. After each skill was presented, students moved into small groups to create examples of that skill. This allowed students to help each other generate ideas and hear the thinking processes of others. For documentation, checklists were created that listed each skill and the date it was taught. Students' work was also used to determine those skills used in mini-lessons. When unit tests were given, it was found that these students performed just as well on tests of basic skills as students in other second-grade classrooms. Thus, it appeared that students in this writing workshop were learning literacy skills using far less instructional time than did other classes while more time was spent writing and composing.

Ms. Baker said that management was going better than she had expected. She put more responsibility on students for correcting tests, organizing the classroom, and choosing writing topics. This made the room more student centered and resulted in her having fewer behavior problems. The time spent teaching routines and procedures led to fewer distractions and helped her workshops run smoothly. Also, creating writing experiences that tapped into students' interests and valued their ideas seemed to contribute to much of her success with classroom management. My observations showed few incidents of off-task behavior during writing workshops. Ms. Baker created structure while giving students choices and a sense of autonomy within this structure.

Notice how the same large blob of text becomes more reader friendly when I insert some headings and add a short introductory paragraph at the beginning. The structure becomes readily apparent and, thus, comprehension is enhanced.

MS. BAKER'S WRITING WORKSHOP

In November 1996, I spent 2 weeks in Ms. Baker's second-grade classroom watching students in her writing workshop. Below are described

(a) the writing process, (b) student talk, (c) teaching skills, and (d) behavior management.

Writing

Here writing was taught as a process consisting of five stages: prewriting, first draft, revising, editing, and publication. Student choice was integral to this process. Ms. Baker said that allowing students to choose their own writing topics seemed to result in a better quality of writing. Students' writing often reflected events going on in their lives, thus increasing feelings of ownership and emotional attachment. They seemed eager to share their ideas and experiences using writing.

Talk

Conversation was an integral part of the writing workshop. Students talked about possible writing topics, about their current writing projects, and about things happening in their lives. More formal conversations related directly to students' writing occurred in individual and small-group conferences and in large-group sharing sessions.

Skills

Skills identified in language arts manuals and unit tests were taught using explicit instruction in short mini-lessons lasting 5 to 10 minutes. After each skill was presented, students moved into small groups to create examples of that skill. This allowed students to help each other generate ideas and hear the thinking processes of others. For documentation, checklists were created that listed each skill and the date it was taught. Students' work was also used to determine those skills used in mini-lessons. When unit tests were given, it was found that these students performed just as well on tests of basic skills as students in other second-grade classrooms. Thus, it appeared that students in this writing workshop were learning literacy skills using far less instructional time than did other classes while more time was spent writing and composing.

Behavior Management

Ms. Baker said that management was going better than she had expected. She put more responsibility on students for correcting tests, organizing the classroom, and choosing writing topics. This made the room more student centered and resulted in her having fewer behavior problems. The time spent teaching routines and procedures led to fewer distractions and helped her workshops run smoothly. Also, creating writing experiences that tapped into students' interests and valued their ideas seemed to contribute to much of her success with classroom management. My observations showed few incidents of off-task behavior during writing workshops. Ms. Baker created structure while giving students choices and a sense of autonomy within this structure.

Using Subheadings to Create More Structure

Subheadings can be used to further organize large sections of text. Subheadings are italicized, flush left, with the first letter of the principal words capitalized. Example:

Skills

Teaching

Skills identified in language arts manuals and unit tests were taught using explicit instruction in short mini-lessons lasting 5 to 10 minutes. After each skill was presented, students moved into small groups to create examples of that skill. This allowed students to help each other generate ideas and hear the thinking processes of others.

Assessment and Evaluation

For documentation, checklists were created that listed each skill and the date it was taught. Students' work was also used to determine those skills used in mini-lessons. When unit tests were given, it was found that these students performed just as well on tests of basic skills as students in other second-grade classrooms. Thus, it appeared that students in this writing workshop were learning literacy skills using far less instructional time than did other classes while more time was spent writing and composing.

CASE STUDIES OR REPRESENTATIVE SAMPLES

Including samples of students' products, quotes, or excerpts from your research journal makes your data come alive. Again, the goal is to convey to the reader a sense of being there.

It's Alive!

When I was doing my doctoral work at the University of Minnesota, I taught writing courses in the composition department. To inform my teaching practice, one quarter I used a technique called dialogue journaling (Watts & Johnson, 1995). I recorded and analyzed my thoughts and feelings after each class on a computer disk (journal). Michelle, a colleague, did the same. At the end of each week we exchanged disks and responded to what the other had written. This had three positive effects: (a) it provided a good sense of what was going on in our classes; (b) it gave us another viewpoint; and (c) we could see how the other was organizing and teaching the writing course. (This is an extremely informative practice and one that I would highly recommend to all teachers.)

Notice below how the inclusion of just a few samples gives you a sense of what I was seeing and experiencing. My entries are in lowercase. Michelle's responses are in uppercase. We both agreed to write without worrying about spelling, grammar, punctuation, or word choice.

1/2/99

Good to start this journal. It is very helpful for me to communicate with somebody else what does and doesn't work and also to hear the triumphs and tribulations of another. It helps also to know what other instructors are doing in their classes and also what they're thinking and feeling. We are human beings dammit!

Also, as teachers of writing we will be practicing what we preach. We will write to see what it is we have to say. We will write to extend and analyze our thoughts. Writing will affect our thinking.

ANDY—THANK YOU FOR ASKING ME TO DO THIS. JUST READING THROUGH YOUR COMMENTS ABOUT THE FIRST WEEK MAKES ME PLEASED TO BE INVOLVED IN THIS VENTURE. I AM LEARNING ALREADY FROM HEARING ABOUT EXPERIENCES YOU'RE HAVING IN YOUR CLASS. THIS IS A GOOD THING.

1/5/99

They're so quiet. Not like my other class at all. I miss the busy bustle of voices when I come into the room. I love to hear students chattering away. I like when students tell me things, tease me gently, or ask me questions. I like when there's a gosh darn relationship. Teaching starts with a relationship. Until then I'm just some clown dancing in front of the classroom.

I have to remember that it's only week 1. It will take me awhile to get there. Students have to learn to trust me and to trust each other. Like petting a strange dog: you have to let him/her smell your hand before you pet him/her.

"Arf!"

Building community—I can't demand instant community. Trust is earned.

ANDY—IT'S THE THIRD WEEK AND MY STUDENTS ARE STILL QUIET AT THE BEGIN-NING OF THE HOUR. THIS BOTHERS ME. I LIKE WALKING INTO A ROOM WHERE EVERYONE IS TALKING, SHARING STORIES ABOUT OTHER CLASSES OR THE COM-MUTE TO SCHOOL. LAST QUARTER WHEN MY STUDENTS WOULD FALL SILENT AS I

CAME INTO THE ROOM, I WOULD SAY, "TALK, TALK. THERE'S NO REASON TO BE QUIET JUST BECAUSE I'M HERE. I WANT TO HEAR YOUR VOICES!" I WOULD SAY THIS LIGHTLY AND IT OFTEN WORKED. BUT LAST QUARTER I TAUGHT IN A SMALL ROOM WITH ONLY THREE ROWS OF DESKS, SO STUDENTS WERE ALREADY CLOSE TO ME AND TO ONE ANOTHER. THIS QUARTER I'M IN A FISH BOWL (302 LIND HALL) WITH MANY ROWS AND A GREAT DEAL OF DISTANCE BETWEEN ME AND THE STUDENTS WHEN I FIRST WALK IN THE ROOM. SOMEHOW I HAVE A LESS EASY TIME MAKING JOKES OR LIGHTENING THE TONE AT THE BEGINNING OF CLASS. ARE YOUR STU-DENTS TALKING MORE NOW?

1/9/99

In group work I allow for chatter-time. Groups are more expensive in terms of time, but the payoff is great in terms of tapping into a diversity of ideas and talents and creating a positive social climate.

My all-female group has done a great job of getting to know each other. I looked up to see them passing pictures around. One of my all-male groups is having a hard time with this. You can insert your own gender generaliza-tions here:

ANDY—I'M EAGER TO KNOW MORE ABOUT HOW YOU BUILD COMMUNITY IN GROUPS. I HAVEN'T STARTED ANY PARTICULAR COMMUNITY BUILDING EXERCISES, ALTHOUGH MOST OF MY GROUPS ARE WORKING OKAY. I'D BE EAGER TO HEAR ABOUT ANY ACTIVITIES YOU HAVE UP YOUR SLEEVE.

PERHAPS YOU COULD ASK YOUR ALL-MALE GROUP TO BE RESPONSIBLE FOR REPORTING BACK TO THE CLASS ON SOME ASSIGNMENT OR FOR MAKING A PRE-SENTATION? MAYBE THEY WOULD BOND THROUGH THE EXPERIENCE OF HAVING TO ASSUME A MORE PUBLIC ROLE IN THE CLASS? I'M NOT SURE.

1/12/99

Ryan is a male student. I read faces pretty well. I got anger from him. He gave me stone face. Sullen, almost challenging at times. I'm beginning to see this as a defense mechanism. He's scared, wondering if he measures up. I know I've sometimes put on a tough exterior to protect my soft inner core . . . Funny the things we do to protect our inner core.

ANDY—I REMEMBER ONE STUDENT FROM LAST QUARTER WHO LITERALLY GLOWERED AT ME. I THINK HE HAD REASON TO BE FRUSTRATED, BUT I COULDN'T FIGURE OUT HOW TO MAKE THINGS BETTER. DON'T YOU WANT TO INTERVENE WHEN YOU SEE A STUDENT LOOKING SO ANGRY? I WANT TO ASK HIM OR HER WHAT'S THE MATTER? BUT THEN I WORRY THAT IT WOULD NOT BE THE PROFES-SIONAL THING TO DO.

1/29/99

So its Monday . . . I'm sure every writing instructor has the same feelings that I'm having this week. Am I doing any good? Are students learning anything? Am I just standing up here wiggling my arms, getting excited for nothing? Are they just nodding their heads like dogs in the back of car windows just so they can get their five credits and move on down the road?

ANDY—IT'S INTERESTING THAT WE'RE BOTH HAVING THESE SAME WORRIES THIS WEEK. IN MY JOURNAL THIS PAST WEEK I MENTIONED THAT TEACHING IS HARD WORK PRECISELY BECAUSE IT IS DIFFICULT TO MEASURE HOW "GOOD" WE ARE. WE DON'T SEE A BUSINESS DEAL GO THROUGH OR CURE A PERSON OF A RASH. INSTEAD, WE HOPE THAT WE'LL PLANT SEEDS . . . OR, EVEN MORE INDIRECTLY, THAT WE'LL FOSTER SOME SORT OF EXCITEMENT ABOUT LEARNING.

Inductive analysis was used to analyze the wealth of data in my dialogue journal. I went through and found the patterns emerging in the types of responses and reported the categories and their frequency. I was then able to report this data in terms of numbers (see Chapter 18). I mixed this with my insights and representative samples to create a good sense of being there.

APPENDICES

Appendices (plural form of appendix) contain information that interrupts the flow of the text. These are placed at the end of your report and comprise information such as data retrieval charts, surveys, questionnaires, tests, interview questions, detailed descriptions that may be too distracting if inserted in the body of your report, or longer samples of your data. Information should be indicated in the body of your text by a reference within parentheses, such as (see Appendix A). As you might have noticed, I have included several appendices at the end of this book.

SUMMARY

- Reporting your findings usually comprises the bulk of your action research report.
- Your data should be converted into a form that can easily be read and understood.
- In writing your action research report the onus is on you to be fair and impartial.
- You are part of the research and should include your thoughts and actions in your report.

- When you write your report, let the readers hear your thoughts as you go through all phases of your research.
- Write as concisely as possible.
- Creating structure using headings and subheadings improves the comprehension of your report.
- Important information that seems to interrupt the flow of your report should be put in an appendix.

QUESTIONS AND ACTIVITIES

1. Find and share a piece of qualitative research related to an area of interest. What do you notice about the writing style?
2. Find and share a piece of quantitative research related to an area of interest. What do you notice about the writing style?

■ ■ ■ ■ ■

FINDINGS: REPORTING QUANTITATIVE DATA USING TABLES, FIGURES, AND GRAPHS

QUANTIFYING REALITY

In an action research report, you may want to describe quantifiable data. In these instances, when do you use numbers and when do you use words to express these arithmetic concepts? The following information is taken from the *Publication Manual of the American Psychological Association* (2001).

Using Numbers

Use numerals to express arithmetic concepts in the following cases:

1. Numbers 10 and above

   The class generated 27 different ideas in the space of 5 minutes.

2. Dates

   This study took place on May 5, 1999.

3. Ages

   She is 7 years old.

4. Time

   The subjects reported to the laboratory at 1:00 P.M. They stayed there for 2 hours and 7 minutes.

5. People in a study

   There were 15 students in this study: 8 males and 7 females.

6. Grade level

   Most children begin grade 2 with a thorough knowledge of consonant sounds.

   (Note: It is grade 2 but *second grade.*)

7. Chapters

   Most would agree that Chapter 17 is the most fascinating chapter of the book.

8. Pages

   Page 1 of this text begins with a fascinating review of the writing process.

9. Scales or rating systems

   He scored a 7 on a 10-point scale.

10. Money

    The subjects in this study were paid $8 for participating.

11. Numbers grouped for comparison with other numbers 10 and above

    The study showed that 9 of 15 students were able to improve their grade averages significantly by learning how to read critically. Of the 15 students participating, 6 received a grade of A, 5 received a grade of B, and 4 received a grade of C.

Using Words

Use words to express arithmetic concepts in the following cases:

1. Numbers below 10

   He sank three of seven free throws.

2. Numbers that begin a title

   Mr. Higgins read the book *Seven Silly Swans* to his second-grade class.

3. Numbers that begin a sentence

   Fourteen children fell asleep during the story.

   (Try to avoid starting sentences with numbers.)

4. Numbers grouped for comparison with other numbers below 10

   In reading class, seven out of the nine boys preferred action stories.

5. Numbers in a hyphenated word

   The Minnesota Vikings are four-time Super Bowl losers.

Reporting Arithmetic Data

Four rules apply for arithmetic data numbers.

1. *Arithmetic data are reported in descending order (from greatest to least).* In the example below, in which some numbers are above 10 (27 walruses), I used numbers instead of words throughout to remain consistent even though some numbers are below 10 (9 kangaroos and 3 white-tailed deer).

   The mosaic contained 27 walruses, 14 elephants, 9 kangaroos, and 3 white-tailed deer.

2. *Tell what you are observing first.*

   This study was designed to determine the types of movie genre that were popular among elementary students.

3. *Tell the total number before you report categories.* Both the examples below are correct. The second one, however, seems a little less repetitive.

   Of 99 total responses, 47 preferred action movies, 31 preferred comedies, 14 preferred science fiction, and 7 preferred historical movies.

   Respondents in this study reported their favorite movie genre. Of 99 total responses, the following preferences were noted: 47 action movies, 31 comedies, 14 science fiction, and 7 historical movies.

4. *Stay consistent with the order of gender or other categories.* Always report numbers in descending order; however, when reporting gender or other categories, the order of the first example must remain consistent throughout. In the example below, I start with the largest total category (Caucasians). The order is 9 males and 2 females. In the categories that follow (Black and Asian), even though the number of females is greater than the number of males, they are reported second to maintain a consistent order.

   There were 28 students in the class: 14 males and 11 females. Nine males and 2 females were Caucasian, 3 males and 7 females were Black, and 2 males and 5 females were Asian.

TABLES

Tables are a quick, visual way to organize and report information. They are especially useful if you have a great deal of numerical data to report. Tables are meant to replace information written in the text. Thus, you might refer to data in the text, but do not duplicate table information in the text. For example, in a study looking at the leisure reading habits of high school students, the following data could appear in the text in written form:

A study was conducted to determine the leisure reading preferences of high school students. Of the 250 students surveyed, 140 were females and 110 were males. The responses were as follows: action or adventure was preferred by 35% of the males and 5% of the females; mysteries were preferred by 10% of the males and 25% of the females; histories were preferred by 0% of the males and 35% of the females; biographies were preferred by 5% of the males and 20% of the females; fantasies were preferred by 20% of the males and 0% of the females; comedies were preferred by 15% of the males and 3% of the females; technical reading was preferred by 5% of the males and 10% of the females; and science fiction was preferred by 10% of the males and 2% of the females. Total responses were as follows: 40% preferred action or adventure, 35% preferred mysteries, 35% preferred history, 25% preferred biography, 20% preferred fantasy, 18% preferred comedy, 15% preferred technical reading, and 12% preferred science fiction.

This paragraph is certainly correct; however, it is not easy to digest this amount of information in this form. A table can be used to report the same information (see Table 18.1). For each gender, the preference is listed from greatest to

TABLE 18.1
Percentages of Leisure Reading Preferences of High School Students

MALES		FEMALES	
Action/adventure	35	Historical	35
Fantasy	20	Mystery	25
Comedy	15	Biography	20
Science fiction	10	Technical	10
Mystery	10	Action/adventure	5
Biography	5	Comedy	3
Technical	5	Science fiction	2
Historical	0	Fantasy	0

TABLE 18.2
Percentages of Leisure Reading Preferences of High School Students

GENRE	MALE	FEMALE	TOTAL
Action/adventure	35	5	40
Mystery	10	25	35
Historical	0	35	35
Biography	5	20	25
Fantasy	20	0	20
Comedy	15	3	18
Technical	5	10	15
Science fiction	10	2	12

least. Use parentheses to refer to a table in the text (see Table 18.1). Because it is a title, the word *Table* is capitalized. In the actual table, the table number should be listed above the table, flush left. The title should be listed on the next line, also flush left. This lets readers know quickly and easily exactly what they are reading. If you are using chapters, merge the table and figure numbers with the chapter numbers. For example, Table 18.1 means Chapter 18, Table 1.

In Table 18.2, the leisure reading preferences of high school students are again reported; however, the data are grouped and listed in descending order according to the genre totals. (Note: Because I referred to Table 18.2 in the sentence, I did not have to put "see Table 18.2" in parentheses.)

Tables help organize information and make it readily available to the reader. Consider the following example:

> This study was conducted to see what kind of footwear middle school students wear. For this study 127 middle school students were observed. The findings are shown in Table 18.3.

TABLE 18.3
Type of Footwear Worn by Middle School Students

TYPE OF SHOE	MALE	FEMALE	TOTAL
Athletic or court shoes	25	20	45
Hiking boots	20	21	41
Sandals	10	20	30
Dress shoes	5	6	11

Figure 18.1.   **Playground games.**

```
PLAYGROUND GAMES
1. Jump rope
2. Soccer
3. Playground equipment
6. Football
7. Chasing games
8. Softball
9. Other
```

FIGURES

Figures include lists, graphs, diagrams, or pictures. Figures are labeled differently than tables. The figure number is italicized, flush left, and followed by a period. In the title, only the first letter is capitalized and the last word is followed by a period (see Figure 18.1). Figures are not the same as tables, and should be counted differently. For example, I have used three tables thus far in this chapter, but this is the first figure, so it is labeled Figure 18.1.

Graphs

Graphs are listed as figures. Bar graphs are used to show comparison. Most word processors have options that allow you to make high-quality graphs quickly and easily. The Vision Quest data described in Chapter 9 is displayed in Figure 18.2. Line graphs are used to show change over time. Figure 18.3 shows how the types of responses in my Vision Quest study changed over time.

Other Visuals

Pictures, photographs, maps, illustrations, or sample products are all examples of figures and should be referred to in the same way as those figures just described. If you have an abundance of these, they should be included in an appendix at the end of your report and simply referred to in the body of your text.

SUMMARY

- Numbers and words are both used to express arithmetic concepts.
- Tables are an effective way to organize information and are especially useful in reporting a large amount of arithmetic data.

Figure 18.2.   **Vision Quest bar graph.**

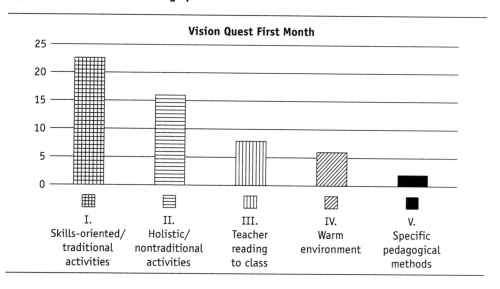

Figure 18.3.   **Vision Quest line graph.**

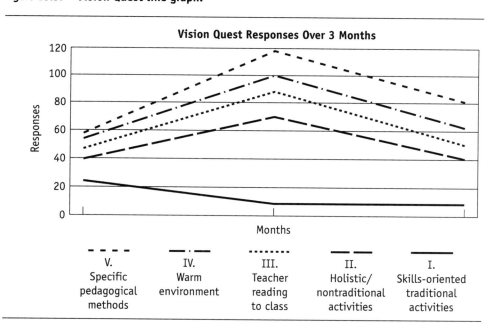

- Do not duplicate table information in the text of your action research report.
- Figures are different from tables and include lists, graphs, diagrams, pictures, photographs, maps, illustrations, and various kinds of examples.

QUESTIONS AND ACTIVITIES

1. Do a quick survey asking at least 25 people to name their favorite book or books. Use inductive analysis to find groups and numbers within each group. Report your data using a table or figure.
2. In the activity above, report your data without using a table or figure.
3. Do a quick survey of at least 25 people to determine their preference for movie genre. Report your data. In your report, describe how the data were collected, what you found, possible differences related to gender, and what that data might mean or how they might be applied.
4. In the activity above, do the same thing except compare adults' preferences to adolescents' (ages 12–19) and children's (ages 6–11).
5. Find an area where you can observe many people. Observe to get a feel for the different kinds of shoes people wear, then find categories and use a data retrieval chart and tally marks to determine what kind of shoe is most often worn. Report your data. In your report, describe how the data were collected, what you found, possible differences related to gender, and what that data might mean or how they might be applied.
6. In the activity above, find a different place to collect the same information. Compare the kinds of shoes worn at the two places.

EPILOGUE

One of the reasons why I am so excited about action research is that it has the potential to change education, to keep our teaching practices evolving. Change is the natural order of things. It is perhaps the only constant in a physical universe that Stephen Hawking (1988) tells us is constantly changing, expanding, moving outward toward chaos and disorder.

To refuse change is the first step in devolution. Thus, we must continue to change and adapt our pedagogical practices to keep pace with the ever-changing needs of our society. Change, however, is not always easy. To leave the safe confines of what is known, to go into the new and unknown, and to allow ourselves to be transformed is to take the heroic journey described by Joseph Campbell (1968). This is the journey that confronts us in our classrooms and throughout our lives.

BELIEF AND FACTS

On top, describe a belief or beliefs related to a particular area or situation. On the bottom, list the facts related to the belief(s).

Belief
Facts

FACTS AND BELIEF

On top, list a set of facts related to a particular area or situation. On the bottom, use deductive logic to describe a belief or beliefs resulting from these facts.

Facts

Belief

EFFECTIVE AND LESS EFFECTIVE

In the T-chart below record the effective and less effective characteristics of an object, event, or procedure.

Effective Characteristics	Less Effective Characteristics

Conclusions:

PLAN TO INVESTIGATE

Investigator: _____

BEFORE THE INVESTIGATION

1. What is your question? What are you curious about? What do you want to investigate?

2. Important background knowledge? Use at least two sources to get information about your question. You may want to interview experts, read books or magazines, or use the Internet.

3. How will you collect data?

read ____	observe ____	checklist ____
weigh ____	measure ____	survey ____
interview ____	time ____	create and test ____
listen ____	count ____	other ____

4. When will you present your findings to the class?

AFTER THE INVESTIGATION

5. Organize your data. (Look for groups or patterns, put it in order, or use tables or graphs.)

6. What conclusions can you make or what interesting ideas do you have based on your data?

7. How will you present your data and conclusions or ideas?

lab report ____	video ____	poster ____
photos ____	plan ____	visual art ____
graph ____	story ____	demonstration ____
brochure ____	speech ____	other ____

CREATIVE PROBLEM SOLVING

Problem:

Ideas:	Best solution:
	Elaborate and refine:

MEANS–END ANALYSIS

End state:

Plan:

Goals:

Current state:

CHECKLIST FOR
SMALL-GROUP CONFERENCES

Group: _____   Date: _____

	yes	no	some
1. The group stayed on task.			
2. Everyone responded or asked a question.			
3. The group used time wisely.			
4. Everyone was prepared for the conference.			

INTERESTING OR IMPORTANT IDEAS
1.
2.
3.

PRODUCT AND PERFORMANCE ASSESSMENT FORM

Student: _____   Age: _____

Grade: _____   Type of Product or Performance: _____

Key: 5 = very high; 4 = high; 3 = average; 2 = low; 1 = very low

When compared to other students of a similar age, rate the product or performance on the following criteria:

1. Creativity _____

2. Integration of ideas ____

3. Technical merit ____

4. Sophistication and level of detail ____

5. Aesthetics: artistic expression, emotion, feeling ____

6. Overall effect ____

Comments:

WRITING ASSESSMENT FORM

Student: _____   Date: _____

Age or Grade Level: _____

Writing prompt:

Key: 5 = very high; 4 = high; 3 = average; 2 = low; 1 = very low

content, ideas _____	mechanics: spelling, grammar, punctuation _____	met deadlines; fulfilled assignment requirements _____
organization, structure _____	fluency, communication _____	appearance _____

Ideas or insights:

Skills to work on:

CHECKLIST FOR INDEPENDENT RESEARCH PROJECTS

Student or Group: _____   Date: _____

Key: 3 = trait is present to a high degree; 2 = trait is present;
1 = trait is present to a low degree; 0 = trait is not present.

____ A question was asked, a problem was identified, or an area of exploration was defined.

____ Data collection was systematic.

____ Data was analyzed in a way that made it credible and trustworthy.

____ The results were described clearly and accurately.

____ Recommendations or conclusions were made based on the results.

____ The research project was linked to a theoretical context.

____ The research was communicated in a way that was understandable.

____ Met all deadlines and requirements.

Focus of the action research:

Major results and conclusions:

REFERENCES

Aamidor, S., & Spicker, H. H. (1995). Promise for the future: Gifted education in rural communities. *Rural Special Education Quarterly, 14*(2), 39–46.

Al-Khalili, J. (1999). *Black holes, worm holes & time machines.* London: Institute of Physics Publishing.

Alkove, L. & McCarty, B. (1992). Plain talk: Recognizing positivism and constructivism in practice. *The Journal of the Association of Teacher Educators, 14,* 16–22.

Allington, R. (2001). *What really matters for struggling readers: Designing research-based programs.* New York: Longman.

American Psychological Association (2001). *Publication manual of the American Psychological Association* (5th ed.). Washington, DC: American Psychological Association.

Armbruster, B. (1993). Science and reading. *The Reading Teacher, 46,* 346–347.

Atwell, N. (1997). *In the middle: New understandings about writing, reading, and learning* (2nd ed.). Portsmouth, NH: Heinemann.

Barone, T., Berliner, D. C., Blanchard, J., Casanova, U., & McGown, T. (1996). A future for teacher education: Developing a strong sense of professionalism. In J. Sikula (Ed.), *Handbook of research on teacher education* (4th ed., pp. 1108–1149). New York: Macmillan Library Reference USA.

Bereiter, C., & Scardamalia, M. (1992). Cognition in curriculum. In P. W. Jackson (Ed.), *Handbook of research on curriculum* (pp. 517–542). New York: American Educational Research Association.

Birman, B. F., Desimone, L., Porter, A. C., & Garet, M. S. (2000). Designing professional development that works. *Educational Leadership, 57,* 28–33.

Bohm, D. (1980). *Wholeness and implicate order.* London: Routledge.

Book, C. L. (1996). Professional development schools. In J. Sikula (Ed.), *Handbook of research on teacher education* (4th ed., pp. 194–210). New York: Macmillan Library Reference USA.

Campbell, J. (1968). *The hero with a thousand faces* (2nd ed.). Princeton, NJ: Princeton University Press.

Chase, W. G., & Simon, H. A. (1973). Perceptions in chess. *Cognitive Psychology, 4,* 55–81.

Chi, M. T., Feltovich, P. J., & Glaser, R. (1981). Categorization and representation of physics problems by experts and novices. *Cognitive Science, 5,* 121–152.

Creswell, (2002). *Educational research: Planning, conducting, and evaluating quantitative and qualitative research.* Upper Saddle River, NJ: Pearson Education, Inc.

Davis, G. A. (1997). Identifying creative students and measuring creativity. In N. Colangelo and G. A. Davis (Ed.), *Handbook of gifted education* (2nd ed., pp. 269–281). Boston: Allyn & Bacon.

Davis, G. A., & Rimm, S. B. (1998) *Education of the gifted and talented* (4th ed.). Boston: Allyn & Bacon.

de Groot, A. D. (1965). *Thought and choice in chess.* The Hague: Mouton.

De Lieon, J., Argus-Calvo, B., & Medina, C. (1997). A model project of identifying rural gifted and talented students in the visual arts. *Rural Special Education Quarterly, 16*(4), 16–23.

Detert, J. R., Louis, K. S., & Schroeder, R. G. 2001. A culture framework for education: Defining quality values and their impact in U.S. high schools. *School Effectiveness and School Improvement, 12,* 183–212.

Dinkelman, T. (1997). The promise of action research for critically reflective teacher education. *The Teacher Educator, 32*(4), 250–257.

Eisner, E. (1983). The art and craft of teaching. *Educational Leadership, 40*(4), 4–13.

Eisner, E. (1998). *The enlightened eye: Qualitative inquiry and the enhancement of educational practice.* Upper Saddle River, NJ: Prentice-Hall.

Erickson, F. (1986). Qualitative methods in research on teaching. In M. Wittrock (Ed.). *Handbook of research on teaching* (3rd ed., pp. 119–161). New York: Macmillan Publishing Company.

Feldman, A., & Atkins, M. (1995). Embedding action research in professional practice. In S. Noffke and R. Stevenson (Eds.). *Educational action research.* New York: Teachers College Press.

Feldman, D. H., Csikszentmihalyi, M., & Gardner, H. (1994). *Changing the world: A framework for the study of creativity.* Westport, CT: Praeger Publishing.

Foshy, A. W. (1998). Action research in the nineties. *The Educational Forum, 62,* 108–112.

Gallagher, J. J. & Gallagher, S. A. (1994). *Teaching the gifted child* (4th ed.). Boston: Allyn & Bacon.

Gambrell, L. B. & Mazzoni, S. A. (1999). Principles of best practice: finding the common ground. In L. B. Gambrell, L. M. Morrow, S. B. Neuman, & M. Pressley (Eds.), *Best practices in literacy instruction*. New York: The Guildford Press.

Gardner, H. (1983). *Frames of mind*. New York: HarperCollins.

Gardner, H. (1996). Reflection on multiple intelligence: Myths and messages. *Phi Delta Kappan, 77*, 200–209.

Gay, L. R., & Airasian, P. (2003). *Educational research: Competencies for analysis and applications* (7th ed.). Upper Saddle River, NJ: Pearson Education, Inc.

Glaser, R. (1984). Education and thinking: The role of knowledge. *American Psychology, 15*, 93–104.

Goodman, K. (1986). *What's whole in whole language?* Portsmouth, NH: Heinemann.

Graves, D. H. (1983). *Writing: Teachers and children at work*. Portsmouth, NH: Heinemann.

Guyton, E., & McIntyre, J. D. (1990). Student teaching and school experiences. In W. Houston (Ed.), *Handbook of research on teacher education* (pp. 514–534). New York: Macmillan.

Hansen, J. (1987). *When writers read*. Portsmouth, NH: Heinemann.

Harman, W. (1998). *Global mind change* (2nd ed.). San Franciso, CA: Berrett-Koehler Publishers, Inc.

Hawking, S. W. (1988). *A brief history of time: From big bang to black holes*. New York: Bantam Books.

Hensen, K. T. (1996). Teachers as researchers. In J. Sikula (Ed.), *Handbook of research on teacher education* (2nd ed., pp. 53–66). New York: Macmillan.

Herbert, N. (1985). *Quantum reality: Beyond the new physics*. New York: Doubleday.

Hodson, D. (1988). Toward a philosophically more valid science curriculum. *Science Education, 72*, 19–40.

Hunsaker, S. L., Abeel, L. B., & Callahan, C. M. (1991). *Instrument use in the identification of gifted and talented children*. Paper presented at the meeting of the Jacob Javits Gifted and Talented Education Program Grant Recipients, Washington, DC. ERIC Document Reproduction Service No. Ed 334 732.

Hursh, D. (1995). Developing discourse structure to support action research for educational reform. In S. Noffke and R. Stevenson (Eds.), *Educational action research*. New York: Teachers College Press.

Imag, D. G., & Switzer, T. J. (1996). Changing teacher education programs: Restructuring collegiate-based teacher education. In J. Sikula (Ed.), *Handbook of Research on Teacher Education* (2nd ed., pp. 213–226). New York: Macmillan.

Johnson, A. (2000). *Up and out: Using creative and critical thinking skills to enhance learning*. Boston Allyn & Bacon.

Johnson, A. (2003a). *A Short Guide to Academic Writing*. Lanham, MD: University Press of America.

Johnson, A. (2003b). *Gifted students and the inner curriculum: Seven literacy techniques to attend to inner dimensions*. Denver, CO: Institute for the Development of Gifted Education.

Knight, S. L., Wiseman, D. L., & Cooner, D. (2000). Using collaborative teacher research to determine the impact of professional development school activities on elementary students' math and writing outcomes. *Journal of Teacher Education, 51*, 26–38.

Krishnamurti, J. (1953). *Education and the significance of life*. San Francisco, CA: HarperCollins.

Leedy, P. D., & Ormrod, J. E. (2001). *Practical research: Planning and design* (7th ed.). Upper Saddle River, NJ: Merrill Prentice-Hall.

Marks, H. M., & Louis, K. S. (1997). Does teacher empowerment affect the classroom? The implication of teacher empowerment for instruction, practice and student performance. *Educational Evaluation and Policy Analysis, 19*, 245–275.

Maslow, A. (1971). *The farther reaches of human nature*. New York: Viking Press, Inc.

McIntrye, D. J., Byrd, D. M., & Foxx, S. M. (1996). Field and laboratory experiences. In J. Sikula (Ed.), *Hand of Research on Teacher Education* (2nd ed., pp. 171–193). New York: Macmillan.

National Center for Educational Statistics (1998). *NAEP 1996 trends in educational progress: Addendum*. Jessup, MD: U.S. Department of Education.

McNiff, J., Lomax, P., & Whitehead, J. (1996). *You and your action research project*. New York: Routledge.

McTaggart, R. (1997). Reading the collection. In R. McTaggart (Ed.), *Participatory action research* (pp. 1–12). Albany, NY: SUNY Press.

McQuillan, J. (1998). *The literacy crisis: Fale claims, real solutions*. Portsmouth, NH: Heinemann.

Metcalf, K., Hammer, R., & Kahlich, P. (1996). Alternative to field-based experiences: The comparative effects of on-campus laboratories. *Teaching and Teacher Education, 12*(3), 271–283.

Miller, J. (1996). *The holistic curriculum*. Toronto: OISE Press, Inc.

Nichol, L. (2003). *The essential David Bohm*. New York: Routledge.

Noffke, S. (1995). Action research and democratic schooling. In S. Noffke and R. Stevenson (Eds.), *Educational action research* (pp. 1–11). New York: Teachers College Press.

Patterson, L., & Shannon, P. (1993). Reflection, inquiry, and action. In L. Patterson, C. Santa, K. Short, & K. Smith (Eds.), *Teachers are researchers: Reflection and action* (pp. 7–11). Newark, DE: International Reading Association.

Perkins, D. N. (1987). Thinking frames: An integrative perspective on teaching cognitive skills. In J. B. Baron & R. J. Sternberg (Eds.), *Teaching thinking skills: Theory and practice* (pp. 41–61). New York: W. H. Freeman.

Piirto, J. (1994). *Talented children and adults: Their development and education.* New York: Macmillan.

Recht, D. R., & Leslie, L. (1988). Effect of prior knowledge on good and poor readers' memory. *Journal of Educational Psychology, 80,* 16–20.

Renzulli, J. S., & Reis, S. M. (1997). The Schoolwide Enrichment Model: New directions for developing high-end learning. In N. Colangelo & G. A. Davis (Ed.), *Handbook of gifted education* (2nd ed., pp. 136–154). Boston: Allyn & Bacon.

Richert, E. S. (1997). Excellence with equity in identification and programming. In N. Colangelo & G. A. Davis (Eds.), *Handbook of gifted education* (2nd ed., pp. 75–88). Boston: Allyn & Bacon.

Routmann, R. (1996). *Literacy at the crossroads: Crucial talk about reading, writing, and other teaching dilemmas.* Portsmouth, NH: Heinemann.

Savage, T., & Armstrong, D. (1996). *Effective teaching in elementary social studies* (3rd ed.). Englewood Cliffs, NJ: Prentice Hall.

Schmuck, R. A. (1997). *Practical action research for change.* Arlingthon Heights, IL: IRI/Skylight Training and Publishing, Inc.

Shulman, L. S. (1986). Those who understand: Knowledge growth in teaching. *Educational Researcher, 15*(2), 4–14.

Smith, F. (1985). *Reading without nonsense* (2nd ed.). New York: Teachers College Press.

Stanovich, K. (1992). *How to think straight about psychology* (3rd ed.). New York: HarperCollins Publishers.

Sternberg, R. (1996). *Successful intelligence: How practical and creative intelligence determine success in life.* New York: Plume.

Sweetland, S. R., & Hoy, W. K. (2002). School characteristics and educational outcomes: Toward and organizational model of student achievement in middle schools. *Educational Administration Quarterly, 36:* 703–729.

Talbot, M. (1991). *The holographic universe.* New York. HarperPerennial.

Taylor, S. J., & Bogdan, R. (1998). *Introduction to qualitative research methods: A guidebook and resource* (3rd ed.). New York: John Wiley & Sons, Inc.

Thelen, J. N. (1984). *Improving reading in science* (2nd ed.). Newark, DE: International Reading Association.

Thomas, K., & Kjelgaard, P. A. (1998). Professional development schools: A review of experiences in eight pioneer sites in Texas. *ERS Spectrum, 16*(1), 41–46.

Tomlinson, C. A. (1995). Action research and practical inquiry: An overview and an invitation to teachers of gifted learners. *Journal for the Education of the Gifted, 18*(4), 468–484.

United States Department of Education (1993). National excellence: A case for developing America's talent. Retrieved from http://www.ed.gove/pubs/DevTalent/part3.htrr

Watts, S., & Johnson, A. (1995). Toward reflection in teacher education: The role of dialogue journals. *Journal of Reading Education, 21,* 27–38.